CRITICAL FLICKER FUSION

Confederation of Independent Psychoanalytic Societies
Boundaries of Psychoanalysis Series
Series editor: Fredric Perlman

CRITICAL FLICKER FUSION

Psychoanalysis at the Movies

William Fried

For Rich,

With esteem and
respect for a fellow
Cineast.

Bill

KARNAC

First published in 2017 by
Karnac Books Ltd
118 Finchley Road, London NW3 5HT

British Library Cataloguing in Publication Data

A C.I.P. for this book is available from the British Library

ISBN 978 1 78220 478 7

Edited, designed and produced by The Studio Publishing Services Ltd
www.publishingservicesuk.co.uk
e-mail: studio@publishingservicesuk.co.uk

Printed in Great Britain by TJ International Ltd, Padstow, Cornwall

www.karnacbooks.com

CONTENTS

ACKNOWLEDGMENTS

The idea of writing psychoanalytically informed essays about films was first suggested to me by Bennett Roth. In the early 1970s, he invited me to participate in a group that met in his home to view and discuss films. He also gave me the opportunity to present my work as a panel member in a course titled "Psycho-Cinema," coordinated at the New School by Arthur Ross, a film historian. Among the other panelists were Bruce Bernstein, Joel Kovel, Everett Dulit, Harvey Greenberg, and Bennett Roth. In addition, he encouraged me to publish an earlier version of the article about *Lord of the Flies* that is included in the present volume. I owe to him the title "Gangsta angst" for the piece on *The Sopranos* in this volume.

A few years later, as a staff member in the psychiatry department of the Maimonides Medical Center in Brooklyn, New York, I was asked and encouraged to contribute papers and presentations about films by William Jeffrey, who had inaugurated a chapter of the Forum for the Psychoanalytic Study of Film at that institution. He received strong support for these events from Marvin Lipkowitz, who was then Chair of the Department of Psychiatry. The films were screened in a large auditorium, and seen by audiences consisting of members of the psychiatry staff, personnel of other hospital departments, the general public, and a scattering of academics and film critics.

Some years later, I served as a board member and officer of Section I (Psychoanalyst Practitioners) of Division 39 (the Division of Psychoanalysis of the American Psychological Association), where I met Albert Brok, a psychoanalyst, film enthusiast, and scholar, who conducted film programs under the auspices of Section I, the Training Institute for Mental Health, and the Argentine Psychoanalytic Association, among others. He, too, invited my participation and contributions.

In sum, then, I wish to express my appreciation to Drs. Roth, Jeffrey, Lipkowitz, and Brok, without whose encouragement I would not have written the essays that comprise the chapters of this book. I also want to thank a number of other colleagues and friends who have supported my writing over the years. They include, Allan Frosch, Helen Gediman, Danielle Knafo, David Lichtenstein, Robert Oelsner, Edna Ortof, Henry Seiden, and Isaac Tylim. I am also grateful to Fredric Perlman and Phyllis Sloate for connecting me to the CIPPS publication process.

Finally, I owe so much to the readers whose warm responses to my work have given me the impetus to keep writing. Among them are Larry Balter, Arnold Breuer, Richard Cohen, Loire Cotler, Beverly Elkan, Dan Fried, Molly Krom, Barbara Lidsky, Victor Otcheretko, George Rehl, Mirel Reich, Irma Seilikovich, Claire Sherr, Margareta Tuckman, Glen Velez, Karen Weiland, and Herbert Weitz.

ABOUT THE AUTHOR

William Fried, PhD, FIPA, is a clinical psychologist, psychoanalyst, photographer, educator, author, and editor. He conducts a practice in psychoanalysis and psychotherapy in his office in Manhattan, near Lincoln Center. Until 2000, he was the Associate Director of Psychiatry Residency Training and the Director of Training and Education at the Maimonides Medical Center in Brooklyn, NY. In those capacities, he participated in the training and education of hundreds of mental health professionals, as a teacher, supervisor, administrator, researcher, scholar, and mentor. In 2000, the Association for Academic Psychiatry named him Teacher of the Year, the first time such an award was given to a non-physician.

Dr. Fried has served as treasurer and president of the board of Psychologist-Psychoanalyst-Practitioners, Section I of Division 39 (The Division of Psychoanalysis) of the American Psychological Association. He also served on the board of Division 39 for twelve years. He is currently a contributing editor of the *DIVISION I REVIEW*, responsible for the Reminiscence feature, a series of articles by and about distinguished contributors to psychoanalysis.

Dr. Fried has published papers on clinical psychoanalysis, psycho-politics, the application of psychoanalysis to the arts, group therapy and group dynamics, psychiatric and psychological education and training, and psychoanalytic theory. He has also written catalogue essays for the exhibits of prominent artists. His own photographs were shown in 2002, 2004, and 2010, in solo gallery exhibits.

Fredric Perlman

"The purpose of playing, whose end, both at the first and now, was and is, to hold, as 'twere, the mirror up to nature; to show virtue her own feature, scorn her own image, and the very age and body of the time, his form and pressure."

William Shakespeare, *Hamlet*; cited in Freud, 1905c, p. 37

"The doctor should be opaque to his patients and, like a mirror, should show them nothing but what is shown to him."

Freud, 1912e, p. 118

I am delighted to offer these prefatory comments to William Fried's new volume, *Critical Flicker Fusion*, the eighth installment in the CIPS book series on the Boundaries of Psychoanalysis. This book is a treat—an engaging and erudite exploration of psychoanalysis and the cinema that is at once entertaining and enlightening. This book is, at the same time, of special importance to the CIPS community, because it is the first volume in our series to focus on the arts and the intimate relationship between psychoanalysis and the arts—an area of intense interest to many analysts, and of special importance to us at CIPS. With this book, William Fried opens a fresh and promising discourse on psychoanalysis and cinema, one that will, I believe, enrich and invigorate the historic relationship between psychoanalysis and art.

The arts, especially literature and drama, played a key role in the discourse of Freud and his followers, and inspired many well-known books and articles devoted to their interpretation. Art has long offered analysts wonderful opportunities to apply emerging insights, illustrate our theories, adduce evidence supporting our ideas, and practice our interpretive skills in public. These endeavors are of value to us and to the larger community. They please us, as well they should. However, we analysts are generally far less mindful of the role of the artist as interpreter of our own experience, the artist as observer of our own lives, indeed, as observers of our own profession. This opens, in my view, a gap between psychoanalysis and the creative arts, a gap that leaves us all the poorer.

One factor that has contributed to this gap has been the drive to professionalize, to establish psychoanalysis as a full discipline on the order of law or medicine. In the United States, this effort eventuated in the "medical orthodoxy", a policy of the American Psychoanalytic Association that restricted formal psychoanalytic training to physicians, excluding from colleagueship not only other mental health professionals, but would-be aspirants from the arts and sciences. The medical orthodoxy thus produced a psychoanalytic world that was limited to physicians, one that differed dramatically from the psychoanalytic community of Europe. In Vienna and the other cities of Europe, the psychoanalytic movement attracted physicians as well as writers, artists, and scholars from a wide range of disciplines whose relationship to the arts, as will be discussed below, was deeply respectful and rooted in traditions of European culture.

Implemented to ensure medical control of psychoanalysis, the medical orthodoxy inspired those it excluded to train themselves, to form small study groups and secure the mentorship of leading European analysts like Theodor Reik, Robert Waelder, and Paul Federn, who had immigrated to the United States on the eve of the Second World War. In the 1950s and 1960s, these analysts and their students formed their own psychoanalytic societies and training institutes based on the multidisciplinary model of European psychoanalysis—and, in keeping with the European traditions, infused with love and respect for the arts.

The Confederation of Independent Psychoanalytic Societies was formed by a small group of these independent societies. We were brought together in the 1980s by a common struggle against the medical orthodoxy. But it was more than professional politics that brought us together. We shared a common commitment to promoting a vision of psychoanalysis as a humanistic enterprise: a cultural movement and a healing discipline informed by its own discoveries as well as the ongoing contributions of a broad spectrum of arts and sciences. This is Freud's precious and enduring legacy. We, the members of the Confederation of Independent Psychoanalytic Societies, are heirs to that legacy.

We must acknowledge here that Freud and the early analysts were not unique in their attitude toward the arts. Many European scientists and physicians of Freud's time were engaged in the arts and wrote about them. Their involvement in the arts reflected their high estimation of the artist as an insightful observer of life and human experience. In his *History of Civilization in England*, a book studied by Freud during his Gymnasium years, Henry Thomas Buckle (1858) observed that the great poets, particularly Homer and Shakespeare, had long been the most astute students of psychology.

In his 1907 essay on Wilhelm Jensen's *Gradiva*, Freud echoed this sentiment, observing that

> creative writers are valuable allies and their evidence is to be prized highly, for they are apt to know a whole host of things between heaven and earth of which our philosophy has not yet let us dream. In their knowledge of the mind they are far in advance of us everyday people, for they draw upon sources which we have not yet opened up for science. (Freud, 1907a, p. 8)

Again, in his introductory comments to "A special type of object choice made by men" (Freud, 1910h) three years later, Freud cited the contributions of creative writers, noting that the creative writer possesses "a sensitivity that enables him to perceive the hidden impulses in the minds of other people, and the courage to let his own unconscious speak." In *The Discovery of the Unconscious*, Ellenberger describes a scene in which Freud, hosting the French playwright Henri-Rene Lenormand in his office, pointed to the works of Shakespeare and of the Greek tragedians on his shelves and comments: "Here are my masters," he said to the playwright, explaining to him [the playwright], that "the essential themes of his theories were based on the intuition of the poets" (Ellenberger, 1970, p. 460)

Kurt Eissler, citing the influence of Shakespeare on Western thought and on Freud, in particular, expresses the same sentiment. In his introductory comments to *Discourse on Hamlet and "Hamlet"*, he writes:

> Shakespeare's educative influence on Western mankind has been and still is enormous . . . Here for the first time—and never since to the same extent repeated—the *full spectrum of man's nature in conflict* was given recognition in a literary universe, not as it appears from a religious or philosophical point of view, but as it is. It was only after Shakespeare that man acquired the freedom to venture into the recesses of the mind, only after him that modern psychology became possible. Indeed, I believe that, with regard to so some essentials, Freud may well have learned more from Shakespeare than he did from his patients. (Eissler, 1971, p. 4)

Eissler's comment is more than a courtesy nod to the community of artists. As the late Martin Bergmann often pointed out in his seminars and in his papers on the psychoanalytic theory of love, Freud's discovery of the Oedipus complex was not Freud's alone but a joint achievement, the product of a collaborative effort by Freud and Sophocles. In his self-analysis, Freud had, to be sure, unearthed buried currents of affection toward his mother and hostility toward his father. But it was Sophocles, Bergmann observed, who interpreted the as yet undiscovered incestuous and murderous desires expressed in these derivative currents of affection and hostility.

The natural "alliance" of art and analysis cited by Freud in his essay on *Gradiva* (Freud, 1907a) clearly reflects the parallel nature of their purposes—to represent some otherwise hidden truth in a form that we can appreciate, absorb, and integrate. The pursuit of truth and the intent to represent it animates every great work of drama and, of course, it is the core and essential aim of psychoanalysis. In this regard, we might imagine art and psychoanalysis as cognate endeavors, joined in their aims and sharing a common ancestry in the classical world of the Greeks, the birthplace of both philosophy and drama.

In considering the meaning of drama and of its contemporary incarnation in the art of film, it is interesting to start with Aristotle's *Poetics*, wherein the philosopher described all drama as "the representation of an action" (Aristotle, 1961, p. 46). By this, he clearly meant people in action, people pursuing the fulfillment of their desires and purposes in accordance with their natures—their characters—and expressing in their action, the thoughts and passions that drive them to act as they do. Drama, as Shakespeare would later write, thus "hold[s] . . . a mirror up to nature" (Shakespeare, *Hamlet*, Act 3, Scene 2), and to our nature as human beings most especially.

Drama, like psychoanalysis, aims to reveal sources of suffering that are hidden from everyday consciousness. Elizabethan writers would characterize these hidden agents of conflict and misery as "imposthumes", abscesses, hidden pockets of putrescence—like the "rottenness" in the state of Denmark or the veiled corruptions of the wealthy and powerful. "Plate sin with gold," Lear cries out, "and the strong lance of justice hurtless breaks" (Shakespeare, *King Lear*, Act 4, Scene 6). Contemporary dramas, like the films discussed in this book, address "abscesses" of a more psychological character: fears, fantasies, false fronts, confusions, and compromises of character that are no less damaging, at least to the individuals involved, than the crimes of Oedipus.

"Every work of drama," William Fried observes, "is driven by secrets." The action of the drama, like the unfolding of an analysis, is shaped by these secrets. In Aristotle's account, the drama culminates in a "recognition" scene where the secret is revealed: the gold-plated abscess is exposed and drained so that health and well-being can be restored to body, soul, and body politic. We might well expand Aristotle's model to include our own recognition experiences, our own insights, as we, audience to the unfolding drama, see our own lives portrayed on the stage or screen, see the imposthumes of our own characters and culture—even if the protagonists portrayed on stage do not. Willy Loman never sees the futile and tragic implications of a life devoted to "name brands"—but we might (Miller, 1989).

William Fried, a psychoanalyst whose background spans both literature and the arts, models an approach to film that enables us to enjoy a fuller measure of insight and of pleasure when taking in a film. I use the term "taking in" intentionally to convey Fried's relationship to the films he discusses. He "takes in" these films much as we "take in" our patients. He pays special attention to the opening scene of each film, much as we ordinarily pay special attention to the patient's first communications or first dream report. He also contemplates the atmosphere of the film, the *mise en scène*, much as we might appreciate the manner, dress, and overall presentation of the patient. Throughout, he engages in an associative process, his thoughts ranging freely from lines of poetry, works of art, philosophical notions, and critical bodies of psychoanalytic theory. Fried's obvious erudition ensures that each association is revelatory, illuminating something hitherto unseen or connecting psychoanalytic theory and cinematic action that expands our understanding of each.

In contemplating Fried's approach, I was reminded of something I had read many years ago in Francis Ferguson's classic study, *The Idea of a Theater*. In this book, Ferguson wrote that becoming acquainted with a play is like becoming acquainted with a person. We see and hear what can be seen and heard, but "instinctively" seek to understand the life that is "both deeper and, oddly enough, more immediate than the surface appearances offer" (Ferguson, 1949, p. 24). Ferguson describes this process as imaginative. As analysts, we might refine this description to include respect, empathy, openness to surprise, and all the other components of an analytic listening process that are evident in Fried's work.

Much like the films described herein, this volume offers both enlightenment and pleasure. I found myself repeatedly surprised to observe the subtle nuances of character, motivation, and meaning that Fried deftly exposes. While I had seen most of these films before reading the book—and enthusiastically echo Fried's recommendation that readers see the films before reading Fried's comments about them—I found that, film after film, Fried's probing and ranging discussions of deepened my "viewing pleasure" as well as my wonderment at the artistry of their creation. While this book will have great value for anyone interested in film and psychoanalysis, Dr. Fried's discussion of psychoanalytic ideas will have particular value to psychoanalysts contemplating a wide range of challenges we face as clinicians—and as human beings.

FOREWORD

Ricardo Ainslie

The magic of film remains fresh more than a century after the initial, flickering forays into what was then an entirely novel medium. Though the days of watching films in grand theater spaces with faux balconies, gargoyles, and art deco architectural details are mostly a thing of the past, for most of us, films retain their sense of wonder. Watching films at home, on trains, or on airplanes, on our television sets, laptops, tablets, or even smart phones, we remain spellbound by this uniquely compelling medium. In *Critical Flicker Fusion*, William Fried helps us understand something about this enduring allure by immersing us in a series of psychoanalytic readings of thirteen films.

The incubation of this art form took shape in the 1890s, just as Sigmund Freud was making his initial, fledgling discoveries about the power of the unconscious and the psyche's complex layers. Both psychoanalysis and film are infused with the sensibilities that defined *fin de siècle* European culture with its intense interest in human subjectivity. Film-makers attempt to capture that subjectivity in ways that might engage audiences, while psychoanalysts attempt to understand that subjectivity by exploring the nuances of human experience and how these play themselves out in "ordinary" and not so ordinary life circumstances. Thus, both film-makers and psychoanalysts work from a shared *weltanschauung*, anchored in the exploration of subjectivity, even as the outcomes of their respective endeavors may differ.

Freud's notion, indeed, dictum, that the study of dreams was the best way to learn about the neuroses and the unconscious has its relevance to film criticism, where approaching a film as if it were a dream allows the analyst to deploy his or her disciplinary tools in order to open a universe of meanings, which otherwise might remain elusive to the movie viewer. Thus we are not surprised when William Fried alerts us, in his introduction to *Critical Flicker Fusion*, that any apparent parallel between his approach to film and psychoanalytic approaches to dreams is decidedly not a coincidence. Fried draws the reader into a unique psychoanalytic space, approaching these thirteen films as if each were an analytic session; inviting us to "watch" as his formulations unfold. Whether the reader is a seasoned psychoanalyst or a die-hard movie buff, Fried's approach is to usher us into an understanding of how a psychoanalyst deciphers the world, be it within a clinical session or at the cinema.

Unlike the typical case presentation, however, where we are given a textual representation of a psychoanalytic process (which is to say, a representation that is always, no matter how elegantly written or faithful in its depiction, at a remove from the experience it is attempting to convey), here, we actually have access to each of the films that are the object of Fried's interest. In this way Fried encourages us to participate in and view the very experiences about which he is writing and thus enter the experiential world he is trying to formulate. The therapeutic parallel would be to actually be sitting in a session, listening to a patient narrate his or her experience, as the analyst puts their understanding of this narrative moment into words. Fried offers the reader the opportunity to actually watch the cinematic "session" as it unfolds and to have a "conversation" with him as he offers us his inferences, interpretations, and understandings.

The complexity of film, with its layers of explicit and implicit, experienced but not necessarily "represented" dimensions, makes film, arguably, unique among the arts. Literature, painting, sculpture, all may draw from symbolism and other elements that give depth and complexity to representation, but film draws from additional qualities that help account for its universal appeal. For example, a master editor may use a palette of visual material in ways that the audience often does not necessarily attend to. That visual palette becomes, quite simply, part of the phenomenological experience of the moment while shaping the experience of the film itself outside of explicit awareness. Music typically moves between the subliminal and the pronounced, at times unnoticed, insinuating itself into the subjective experience of the film, at others quite salient and defining. The power of pacing, and the editor's use of it to regulate the experience of the viewer is also something that often forms a kind of "un-thought known" in the viewer's encounter with the film. Further, a film's other visual qualities, the cinematography, the staging, lighting, and perspective, all give film a dimension that is unique to this medium. None of these elements are accidental, and they contribute to the experiential fabric of a film in ways that can be largely unconscious.

The quality that most distinguishes film from other art forms, however, the element that most accounts for film's magical quality, is that films, and the characters within them, literally move in time. It is this temporal dimension that stunned audiences at the end of the nineteenth century upon first encountering the flickering images on a screen, moving at sixteen frames per second (the threshold at which the image appeared to be truly in motion as opposed to a series of staggered still images). The fact that we follow characters as they move through time helps approximate lived experience in ways that are unique. Text on the page, color and form in painting, or the materials and contours of sculpture may all be deeply compelling and profoundly meaningful, but, with few exceptions, they are ultimately visually static. The miracle of film is that it transcends that limitation, giving us real-time movement in which we "see," quite directly, the actions of characters and we witness their verbalizations as they move through time and space. There is something about these properties that facilitates our engagement with a film's characters and, by implication, with ourselves. In this way, film is the art form that most closely resembles the complexities of the human psyche as we literally see characters behave and engage life.

Both William Fried's artistry and intellect are in considerable evidence throughout this book. His insights about these thirteen films draw not only from his many years of experience as a practicing psychoanalyst, but also from his earlier life as a professor of literature. The roles of psychoanalytic interpreter and literary critic merge seamlessly in this effort, not in pedantic, overly and self-consciously abstracted readings, but in fresh, intimate encounters with each of these thirteen films. Fried clearly loves etymology and word play as much as he loves plumbing the depths of human motives and applying psychoanalytic constructs to what he sees. Moving us through each film, he describes characters, settings, and plot lines, showing the reader the power of close readings and of psychoanalytic ideas to help elucidate them. In doing so he gives us what is essentially a hybridized interpretive methodology—part psychoanalysis, part literary criticism, part film criticism—all working close to the ground, as it were. We witness through Fried's method the power of a psycho-analytic sensibility applied here to the world of film, but what is readily evident is that psychoanalysis retains a unique capacity for understanding the complexity of human experience more generally.

Introduction:
The films, the method, the themes

This book consists of a collection of essays about feature films regarded from the perspective of psychoanalysis. I wrote these essays for presentations at conferences where, first, the films were shown in their full length to afford the audiences the vividness and immediacy of their imagery and language. The audiences were, thus, ready to form their own impressions before listening to mine and then engaging in a general discussion. I think readers of this book will also find it most valuable and pleasurable if they see the films as shortly before reading about them as possible.

The essays that comprise the chapters of the book were written over a span of some twenty years. Reading them all recently, I think I discerned a gradual improvement in their conception as well as in my prose. When I wrote the early ones, I regarded myself as an amateur, albeit a somewhat gifted one, but with no special training or expertise in film. I did know something about explicating texts, both from being a psychoanalyst and from skills and knowledge I had acquired to ply my earlier profession as a teacher of English. I have, since, learned a little bit more about films, but my principal interest is in their meanings and not the technical elements by and of which they are made.

Many of the films were selected by the person who had organized the meeting at which they were to be presented, so, often, they were given to me as an assignment. In some cases, I had never even seen the film before preparing it for presentation. This was true, for example, of *The Conversation, Notes on a Scandal, Up in the Air, An Affair of Love,* and *Lord of the Flies.* Among the films I chose myself, were *Talk to Her, Blade Runner, Gods and Monsters,* and the two episodes of *The Sopranos.*

Interpreting a film is like interpreting any other work of the imagination, including the speech and behavior of analysands in their treatment sessions. What it requires is a comprehensive take on the material that makes sense of as much of it as possible. When psychoanalysts interpret films, however, they tend to treat the characters as though they were real people, and analyze the unconscious sources of their behavior, or they tend to regard the film as an autobiographical document in which the personality of the auteur may be analyzed. I think analysts would do greater justice to movies if they approached them as they do sessions, that is, as potentially coherent, internally consistent entities, the underlying meanings of which can be discovered by a process of exegesis. This, at least, is the method I use in the book.

I have written essays about thirteen films, in all, and put them into four categories: Secrets, Time and Death, Love and Lust, and Human Identity. The category Love and Lust, contains four exemplars and the others contain three each, films that are built on the essential theme. Secrets, for example, includes *Notes on a Scandal* (Eyre, 2006), *The Conversation* (Coppola, 1974), and *The Sopranos* (Chase, 2000). Obviously, however, each film may also have a subtheme of sufficient significance to be discussed under a category other than its own. For example, though I have adjudged *Blade Runner* (1982), to be, first, a study of human identity, one way the study is pursued is in the love affair between Rick, a presumed human, and Rachael, who may be a Replicant.

In thinking and writing about each film, I have tried to adhere to the discipline known among literary critics as close reading. Be it known, however, that they neither invented it nor have been its preeminent practitioners. That honor probably belongs to the Talmudists of the Greco-Roman period, some of whom may have been the rabbis to whom Jesus listened and spoke in the Temple when he was twelve years old. It would not be too great a stretch to regard Freud either as a latter day Talmudist or, at least, as a principal beneficiary of that tradition.

The method calls for minute examination of the visual and kinetic components, and the auditory constituents (both verbal and non-verbal), to determine how they contribute to the meaning of the film. Film culture provides a term for the comprehensive impression that these create: it is *mise en scène*. In experiencing the *mise en scène*, I seek a pattern of internal consistency that will result in an elucidation of the work's themes and motifs. I try to approach the film with as few preconceptions as possible and allow its materials their sway, in the hope that, at some point in the process, I shall be able to form a few hypotheses about it and find out whether they are valid for the work as a whole.

Any kinship that may be noted between this way of working with films and the class of practices used by psychoanalysts with dreams and other clinical materials is neither accidental nor unintended. Although there are differences according to the intrinsic nature of each product, films, sessions, and dreams have enough in common that the methods used to interpret any tend to be relevant to all.

*To the memory of my dear friend and
close reader, Gary Tuckman*

CHAPTER ONE

Secrets

E very work of drama is driven by secrets. They are the source of suspense in all detective stories and of pathos and compassion in high tragedy. The vast domain of narrative that lies between those two genres—detective stories and high tragedy—is also impelled by unknowns that must be discovered. Of the films discussed here, *Notes on a Scandal* (Eyre, 2007), *The Conversation* (Coppola, 1974), and the two episodes of *The Sopranos* (Chase, 2000) are most illustrative of such unknowns.

Barbara and Sheba, the protagonists of *Notes on a Scandal* share the secret that Sheba is sexually involved with Steven, her student. But Barbara also maintains and lives in a secret world that she entrusts only to her journals. After Barbara has coerced from Sheba a pledge to discontinue the affair with Steven, Sheba keeps her meetings with him secret. Beneath these, however, are unconscious secrets related to anxiety about aging and death that remain inaccessible to the two women even as they incite their aberrant behavior.

Surveillance is the central trope of *The Conversation*. To "surveil" is to observe someone or something, most often secretly: that is, without the knowledge or consent of the observed. The purpose of the observation is to pry into matters that the observed prefers to keep private.

In essence, it is the secretive attempt to penetrate secrets. This is the realm of voyeurism, the wish to see or witness what is taboo or forbidden. Its prototype in early childhood is curiosity about the sexual organs of parents, and the uses to which they are put.

Harry Caul, the protagonist of *The Conversation*, is a surveillance professional, regarded by his colleagues as "the best in the business." The film is about the secrets he has been hired to ferret out, but, more pointedly, about the secrets he harbors unconsciously that derive from an especially violent set of childhood oedipal fantasies.

The species of secret that drives *The Sopranos* is a function of its being a series about a fundamentally secret organization, known popularly as the Mafia. Accordingly, almost all the action is conducted in secrecy. Within the perimeter of this overriding secret, however, there are myriad other secret enclaves and operations. Of special interest among them are Tony's confidential psychotherapy sessions with Dr. Melfi, and, in turn, hers with her supervisor/therapist, Elliot Kupferberg. From the dramatization of these relationships, we are able to infer a great deal about the unconscious wishes of the principal characters and their reasons and methods for hiding them from themselves.

Notes on a Scandal: Transgression

To begin with, I believe the film is about a transgression that carries personal, psychodynamic, cultural, and mythic significance. I am referring to Sheba's sexual affair with Steven Connolly. The affair and its surrounding events evoke and draw from a rich literary tradition that includes works by Joseph Conrad, Dostoyevsky, and T. S. Eliot. At the level of myth, it taps Biblical, classical, and folkloric sources. Among the psychodynamic elements that animate the characters are unconscious fantasy, internal object representations, and projective identification. Psychoanalysis, group dynamics, and sociology contribute much to the development and understanding of the powerful central theme—that of boundaries and their violation.

I set great store on the beginning of films and sessions, on what, in the world of opera, is called the overture, because I believe it contains a condensation of what will turn out to be the essence of the work. In *Notes on a Scandal*, it consists of a shot of Barbara, seated alone, on a bluff overlooking the city. Names, as we shall see, are a key to deciphering the film. Barbara is derived from an ancient Greek origin. It means foreign, or strange. Her solitary position above it all is consistent with her name. In a voice-over, she says, "People have always trusted me with their secrets."

The scene shifts abruptly to a close-up of Barbara's pen, journal, and a cigarette smoldering in an ashtray. Her voice-over continues, "But who do I trust with mine? You. Only you." She is referring to her journal. The camera then pans to a shelf heavy with completed journals, the spine of each marked with a sticker indicating its date. There are scores of them. She has been doing this for a long time. Here, the title of the film is displayed against the background of the journals. "Notes on a Scandal," it reads, the first three words in white, the fourth in lurid red. The emphasis is on the notes. Barbara is a chronicler: she teaches history and she keeps a record. But the record she keeps is distorted and tendentious, akin to that of an earlier model, Dostoyevsky's underground man, whose metier is almost a pure culture of spite and who, like Barbara, lives in a basement in what he calls his funk hole, where he pens an acid critique of his fellow humans (Dostoyevsky, 1992).

Another passage that resonates with Barbara's preoccupation with secrets is the epigraph at the start of "The Love Song of J. Alfred Prufrock" that T. S. Eliot (1950a) borrowed from Dante. In it, Guido da Montefeltro, an inmate of Hell, says that if he believed he were confessing his crimes to anyone who might return to the world of the living, he would refrain from speaking, but since he is sure that no one ever returns from Hell, he resolves to disclose his secrets without fear of infamy. The irony, of course, is that not only does Dante return, but also he bruits Guido's story abroad in a poem read by millions, along with intimate accounts of several other inmates of the netherworld.

This irony applies equally to the secrets contained in Barbara's journals, divulged later in the film, to the "confidential" material of psychoanalytic sessions routinely shared with supervisors, at conferences, and—even less justifiably—in more casual conversations; and, in the end, to much that people may wish to conceal but, for unconscious reasons, are unable to.

It soon becomes apparent that Barbara sees herself as above and superior to her students and colleagues. She stands at the window over the entrance to the school, observing and being critical of those who arrive, referring to them as "Local pubescent proles, the future plumbers and shop assistants, and doubtless the odd terrorist, too." In this scene, her absorption in the significance of class is introduced, to be elaborated and fleshed out later. Next, we are given a demonstration of Barbara's unequivocal authority over the seemingly uncontrollable behavior of her adolescent students. She has not ended her lesson when the bell rings signaling the end of the period. The students rise to leave. Turning to them from the board she has been writing on, her Medusa gaze arrests their departure and returns them all to their seats. Then, with a barely perceptible nod, she releases them from her spell and they regain their ability to move.

Barbara's predilection for matters of class is further illustrated in her observations about Sheba, whose late and, therefore, conspicuous entrance to the staff meeting has drawn her attention. She speculates about Sheba, "Is she a sphinx or simply stupid? Artfully disheveled today. The tweedy tramp coat is an abhorrence. It seems to say, 'I'm just like you,' but clearly she's not." She adds, "A fey person I suspect. Fey." In addition to her disapproval of Sheba's dressing down to gain the acceptance of her working class students, she applies the word "fey" to her with special emphasis. The several definitions of "fey" are acutely instructive. It can mean "Giving the impression of vague unworldliness; having supernatural powers of clairvoyance; fated to die, or on the point of death; and marked by a foreboding of death or calamity" (*Oxford Dictionaries Language Matters*, 2016)

Barbara's own powers of clairvoyance are relevant here since she has already displayed an uncanny degree of control over an age group and class notorious for being unruly, and she will, as the film progresses, exhibit a range of other gifts typically ascribed to witches. She seems to be foreseeing that Sheba will bring disaster, that her vague unworldliness contains and conceals this dangerous quality, and wishfully thinking that the feyness she attributes to her constitutes an affinity with her own occult dispositions.

Likewise, the word *sphinx* that Barbara applies to Sheba is not randomly chosen. The Theban Sphinx, with whom we are familiar from the tale of Oedipus, was a woman who asked people riddles. If they could not solve the riddles, she killed them. Coincidentally, the Queen of Sheba, who came to visit King Solomon, brought precious gifts and several riddles with which to test his wisdom. He passed the test. For Barbara, Sheba is a riddle and a dangerous one, since she answers a deep and enduring longing that is central to Barbara's existence, one that she does not understand. Like the Biblical queen, Sheba possesses great wealth, which, along with her patrician background, is fascinating to Barbara.

Her next comment about Sheba's effect on the school—"She has certainly rippled the waters of our stagnant pond. They flock to her. Even limp little Brian had a go. Oh the horror"—ends with a famous quotation from Joseph Conrad's *The Heart of Darkness* (2008, p. 147): the dying words of its central character, Kurtz. Barbara seems to detect a parallel between Kurtz, a successful and wealthy ivory trader who captivated and exploited the Africans among whom he lived, and Sheba, who is in the process of captivating the students and faculty of the school. Kurtz's transgression was to violate boundaries of race, class, and sexuality. Marlow, who tells Kurtz's story, inherits the role of the "Secret Sharer" (2012), the eponymous Conrad work that is invariably published as a companion piece to *The Heart of Darkness*. As we have already observed, Barbara is a quintessential sharer of secrets and she later becomes privy to the one in which Sheba reveals her own transgressions of class, age, and law.

Presently, Barbara again displays an ability to control the students' behavior and set limits, which borders on the uncanny. With the single word "Enough!" she stops the *mêlée* that Sheba has been caught in. When she then says, "Outside!", all the students leave. She follows this with a remarkable demonstration of occult powers when she forces Steven Connolly to break the adolescent version of the Code of Omerta by using an incantation. She says, "Yes. Brain. Mouth. Speak," and magically, Steven, who a moment before told her he did not know why he was fighting with another boy, blurts out the lewd reason with no hesitation.

Suddenly, however, this intelligent, sophisticated, cynical, worldly-wise enchantress becomes a naïve, star-struck acolyte of the very person on whom she has been privately passing such severe judgment. The change is abrupt and, therefore, requires that we account for it within the context of the story. In hindsight, we might say that it was occasioned by Barbara's developing hope that she would be able to engage Sheba in the kind of relationship that satisfies the requirements of her inner script. This would certainly be accurate, but I believe there is something else, and the film provides a clue to its nature by showing Barbara's elaborate preparations for her luncheon visit to Sheba's home. As a conscientious member of the middle class,

Barbara fulfills a set of time-honored conventions for a social encounter with the rich: she shops for a new outfit, has her hair done, stops at the florist for a bouquet, and in general, to quote Polly, gets "All poshed up." She is very anxious at the door and, profoundly humiliated when Polly asks whether she is going somewhere, she replies lamely that she has an appointment. "Later. In town." Unrelieved of her bouquet, she holds it awkwardly on her lap.

The entire scene seems designed to underscore Barbara's subjugation to the protocols of class. When Sheba later confides much about her personal life and history, Barbara says, "It's a peculiar trait of the privileged: immediate, incautious intimacy," and sharpens this to, "But Sheba went well beyond the tendencies of her class. She was utterly candid. A novice confessing to the Mother Superior." Her emphasis here is on the class-specific carelessness of Sheba's almost cavalier self-disclosure, on her own capability to elicit the secrets of others, and on her role as a guardian of societal values.

The close of that day finds Barbara at her writing, pasting a gold star to the end of her account of it and declaring, "I always knew we'd be friends. Our mutual reserve inhibited us, but now it is manifest, a spiritual recognition." She feels the special elation that always results when an external event or person seems to confirm and validate a crucial unconscious scenario. As her voice-over speaks these thoughts, the camera angle shifts abruptly from a close-up of her very pleased expression, to a long shot from behind her, the middle distance occupied by Portia, her cat, who, in the mores of witchcraft, is her familiar spirit, or simply familiar, a personal demon in the form of an animal that assists the witch in her sorcery. The name Portia immediately recalls the character in Shakespeare's *Merchant of Venice*; it is less familiar as a genus of hunting spiders that prey on other spiders, especially those that build and live in nests. Barbara's familiar, then, epitomizes her unconscious fantasy of appropriating the desirable qualities of someone she admires. Towards the end of the film, after the rupture in her relationship with Sheba, she writes, "They always let you down in the end. Jennifer said I'm too intense, meaning what, exactly? That I am loyal in my friendships? That I will go to the ends of the earth for someone I admire?"

After Barbara discovers Sheba's affair with Steven, she becomes the custodian of boundaries, insisting that even Sheba's individual tutorial with him constituted a breach of structure and a prospective threat to the stratified order of society. In an earlier conversation, one of the veteran teachers admonishes Sheba, "If we pull strings for one child, the entire system will unravel." The affair, then, is no mere impropriety of one misguided person, with restricted local consequences; rather, it ramifies to the prevailing taboos on class relations within British society and—both historically and in our globalized contemporary situation—on relations between English people, those whom they colonized in the past, and those with whom they trade, influence, and exploit in the present. That Steven Connolly is Irish is not accidental in this connection. Less than two centuries ago, Jonathan Swift wrote a scathing satire titled "A Modest Proposal" (2009, pp. 230–239) in reproof of England's brutality to the Irish. In it, he suggests that poverty in Ireland would be alleviated if parents were to sell their children to be slaughtered and eaten for food. He goes on to provide recipes for the preparation and cooking of the children's tender flesh. There is a comparable, if less grisly, sense in which Sheba consumes Steven.

Consider the following quotation from Freud's (1912–1913) *Totem and Taboo* in relation to the significance of Sheba's trespass and Barbara's response:

> It is equally clear why it is that the violation of certain taboo prohibitions constitutes a social danger which must be punished or atoned for by all the members of the community if they are not all to suffer injury. If we replace the unconscious desires by conscious impulses we shall see that the danger is a real one. It lies in the risk of imitation, which would quickly lead to the dissolution of the community. If the violation were not avenged by the other members, they would become aware that they wanted to act in the same way as the transgressor. (1912–1913, p. 33)

A passage more apposite to the theme of *Notes on a Scandal* would be difficult to find.

Only when Sheba succumbs to her desire for Steven do we grasp that boundary violations are only a part of the conflict that motivates the action. The violations of legal, class, and generational boundaries are, themselves, driven by a compulsive hunger for the vitality, beauty, passion, carelessness, and sheer prodigality of youth. Almost every character in the film lusts for someone younger: Richard for Sheba, Barbara for Sheba, Sheba for Steven, Pete for Polly, Barbara for

Jennifer Dodd and Annabel, the woman she picks up at the end of the film.

The quest for youth, then, is the overarching theme of the film, and the dynamics of the individual characters are both secondary to, and supportive of, it. That Barbara envies and wishes to consume Sheba is clear, just as it is clear that Sheba strives, symbolically, to consummate an incestuous relationship with her father by seducing Richard away from his wife.

Let us recall that Sheba's full name is Bathsheba. In the Bible, she was the wife of Uriah the Hittite and she had an adulterous relationship with King David. To facilitate their affair, David contrived to have Uriah killed in battle. The name Bathsheba means the daughter of wealth. Sheba Hart, like her Biblical namesake, becomes the lover and then the wife of an older, accomplished man. Hart, incidentally, was the medieval name given to a mature deer, worthy of being hunted by nobles, a so-called beast of venery, the latter from a Latin root meaning both "hunt," and "Venus." Richard's nickname for Sheba is "Bash," signifying, alternatively, a party and a destructive act. I need hardly comment on the aptness of Barbara's surname, Covett.

If the foregoing paragraphs justify my assumption that the striving for youth is the key to this film, it must follow that the people in it experience the passage of time as intolerable. Perhaps this is why most of the sex scenes between Sheba and Steven take place on the ground between two railroad cars, with a ubiquitous sound of passing trains as background. Thus, their union is juxtaposed with a vivid symbol of elapsing duration that recalls the famous poem "To His Coy Mistress" that Andrew Marvell (1989, pp. 478–479) wrote in the seventeenth century:

> Had we but world enough and time,
> This coyness, Lady, were no crime . . .
>
> But at my back, I always hear
> Time's wingèd chariot hurrying near;
> And yonder all before us lie
> Deserts of vast eternity.
> Thy beauty shall no more be found;
> Nor, in thy marble vault, shall sound
> My echoing song; then worms shall try
> That long-preserved virginity,

And your quaint honor turn to dust,
And into ashes all my lust;
The grave's a fine and private place,
But none, I think, do there embrace.
Now therefore, while the youthful hue
Sits on thy skin like morning dew,
And while thy willing soul transpires
At every pore with instant fires,
Now let us sport us while we may . . .

In deliberate contrast to the film's dramatization of Sheba's desperate gesture to conquer time is the image of Barbara's hand, a bit tremulous, veiny, and conspicuously aging, with the ubiquitous cigarette between her fingers, covering that of Sheba as she assures her, "I'm not going to report you. I want to help you, to support you through this." Barbara's smoking cigarettes is a leitmotif throughout the film, part witch's stock-in-trade of smoke and ash, part poisonous sustenance: whenever Barbara needs soothing, she draws deeply, greedily, on a cigarette. Strangely and significantly, though Barbara inhales the smoke deeply, she never exhales it, reinforcing the impression that smoke is her indigenous nutriment. During their heated argument after Sheba has discovered Barbara's journals, Barbara practically spits at her the phrase, "You're not young!" An additional delineation of Barbara's negation of youth is her pointing out, first to Sheba, and then to Annabel, the residue of milk on their faces, evidence of their innocence and wholesomeness that seems to pain her.

Further development of this theme occurs when Sheba chooses to attend Ben's performance as a wizard rather than accompany Barbara in her farewell to Portia. As a child with Down syndrome, Ben will never age. His role as a wizard is the effective contrast to Barbara's as a witch with Portia as her familiar. Sheba opts for Ben's white magic over Barbara's black, for his eternal innocence over Barbara's corruption and Portia's death. Until this moment, Sheba has been profoundly ambivalent towards Ben because his youth and innocence are devoid of beauty and excitement. Instead, she has clutched at Steven's adolescent vitality and allure, and discovered, to her dismay that, far from artless, he has played her guilefully.

Barbara assumes Sheba will seek her solace after Steven repudiates her. As a result, she resolves to forgive Sheba, declaring to herself, "Her betrayal hurt me more than I dare show but I will forgive her and heal

myself in private. She's worth it, this one. She's the one I've waited for."
The speech conveys Barbara's inherent narcissism, her Fairbairnian
(1952) strategy of importing all experience to her inner world where
she can subject it to the radical distortion and reorganization required
by her private script. Her reference to "this one," renders Sheba one of
the several actors she has auditioned to play the central character in
her core drama, albeit a prime candidate for the role, one whose dressing room door might be adorned with a gold star. Apropos gold stars,
however, this scene is intercut with one of Sheba working on Ben's
wizard hat, to which she is affixing stars and crescent moons in gold
paper, the juxtaposition of poison and antidote.

Even as Sheba is violating generational, sexual, and legal boundaries with Steven, she is remarkably successful at preserving and
defending her boundaries with Barbara. This is most clearly shown in
the scene in which she refuses to allow Barbara to complete the hyp-
notic spell she is casting by stroking Sheba's arms. It is also evident in
Sheba's choosing Ben's play over Portia's death.

Barbara's power, a function of her control over secrets, is broken
when she shares with Brian the secret involving Sheba's affair. She
does this immediately following the death of Portia, her familiar, and
symbol of her occult authority. A kindred process occurs in psychoanalysis, when the strength of a symptom is reduced as its unconscious sources are brought to light. The loss of her power is under-
scored by her barely being able to close the door of her apartment
against the intrusion of Steven, whereas earlier her command of such
boundaries was absolute. It is also reflected in a visual pun in the
scene in which Sheba's discovery of Barbara's use of gold stars begins
on the privy.

The Ancient Greeks had two words for time: *chronos*, denoting
ordinary, sequential time, and *kairos*, meaning the right moment,
when the extraordinary event occurs, more like the suspension or
arrest of time. I think this film is about the pursuit of *kairos* as an
attempt to overcome the terrors of aging and death.

The end of *Notes on a Scandal* finds Sheba going upstairs and
Barbara, down. Sheba is the rich girl; Barbara is the alien. Barbara has
failed in her effort to redeem the time, to resolve the *kairos* problem by
linking with Sheba. She has not succeeded in acquiring life from
Sheba's touch. Recall her thoughts while bathing:

People like Sheba think they know what it's like to be lonely. But of the drip, drip . . . of long-haul no-end-in-sight solitude . . . they know nothing. What it's like to construct an entire weekend around a visit to the launderette . . . or to be so chronically untouched . . . that the accidental brush of a bus conductor's hand . . . sends a jolt of longing straight to your groin.

She returns to the underground, where her core function is to create a record, a history, a chronicle of her futile quest for gold-star events.

Sheba has failed in her attempt to reverse time, and resumes her place in its inexorable progression. If the thought attributed to Kafka (2016, see www.goodreads.com), that the meaning of life is that it ends, has any validity, then the problem of time is the triad of youth, aging, and death. The problem is richly symbolized in Tithonus, in Greek mythology the lover of Eos, the goddess of the dawn. In Tennyson's eponymous poem (1933), Tithonus asks Eos for immortality; with the help of Zeus, she confers it on him. But he forgets to ask for eternal youth and, as a result, must age but cannot die. He longs for death. Because he continues to age, his experience of time is linear, but time for his lover, Eos, is cyclical.

It is *kairos* that redeems the time from its unalterable linearity. Humans deal with endings by creating eschatology, monuments (including estates and progeny), procrastination, and sequels. Endings are intolerable. They must be eradicated from experience by the next big thing—the hereafter, the children, the foundation, and the work of art or science. Another antidote that all psychoanalysts are familiar with is the serial repetition of stereotyped behavioral scripts that render the lives of patients spuriously cyclical.

Barbara's life is recorded but unexamined. As a result, she is doomed to repeat her inner script as we see her doing with Annabel in the final scene. Sheba's life is lived but unexamined. She goes back to Richard and her family. This, too, is a repetition.

But the events between the attempts and the failures constitute the narrative, the story, the film, the tale told by the idiot or maybe the genius, full of sound and fury, signifying either nothing or something. If it is like this film, it is a cautionary tale. It says that enactment is not enough, that transformation requires reflection, that *kairos* always involves a tacit acknowledgement of endings.

The Conversation: Listening with a fourth ear

The theme of eavesdropping, voyeurism, and spying on others is an elaboration of the scoptophilic wish to gain forbidden knowledge of parents' activities in the primal scene. That this pattern of motivation underlies Harry Caul's behavior is evident from the very beginning, and throughout *The Conversation*, by the predominance of phallic images at critical moments. For example, the obelisk in Union Square Park during the opening credits, the phallic shape in front of the director's building, the phallus on the coffee table in Harry's apartment, the phallic post on the staircase in the hall of Amy's building and the mural depicting Quoit Tower in the hotel room. Indeed, the problem with this film is its heavy-handedness and lack of subtlety. Coppola lays on symbolism with a trowel as though he fears that we will miss his meaning; one reason, I suppose, that this film is beloved of psychoanalysts.

The primal scene is almost always covered by a screen memory. In Harry's case, it is conveyed in a dream. He tells the woman whose conversation he has been bugging that his legs were paralyzed when he was a child, that while giving him a bath, his mother was called away by someone at the door, and that he nearly drowned. Later, he hit his father's friend in the stomach and the man died. The oedipal theme of his mother's leaving him for a rival makes him feel as though he is drowning. The paralyzed legs (no doubt a conversion symptom) are a symbolic castration, and he succeeds in murdering the father symbolically by ramming his head into the man's stomach, using his entire body as a destructive phallus.

The waking experience prior to the dream is a party in Harry's shop. Something about his current job is stirring up a painful childhood conflict, one that Harry has managed to keep in check by using an array of dissociative and paranoid defenses. The pressure of emerging painful memories and dormant wishes leads him to permit an unharacteristic invasion of his private space: he invites, or tolerates the presence of professional competitors, colleagues, and women in his shop. By allowing this intrusion, he sets the stage for self-discovery.

The phrase, "Somebody's baby boy," originally used by the woman in Union Square Park to describe a vagrant lying on a bench, takes on a very personal meaning as a peculiarly passive Harry is put to bed, soothed, and made love to by a middle-aged, married woman. As he lies in bed about to commit symbolic incest, he recalls two other phrases used by the cheating couple: "He'd kill us if he had the chance," and "Oh God, what I've done!" The soundtrack of his dream consists of the inchoate syllables of the voices on his undeciphered tape.

In the dream, he tries to undo the damage that his surveillance of the couple might cause by confessing to the woman. This is consistent with his defensive misinterpretation of the situation he is observing. Identifying with the young man, he assumes that the adulterous couple are in danger from the jealous husband. He misses their intention to kill the husband because it comes too close to his childhood wish to murder his father. Ironically, history repeats itself, as the woman whose "baby boy" he became betrays him by absconding with his secrets, the tapes. That he deals with women as either idealized or denigrated is reflected in his reluctance to shatter the figure of the Virgin in his frantic search to find the listening device that has been placed in his apartment.

In folklore, the child born with the caul (the inner fetal membrane, especially when it covers the head at birth) is considered destined for greatness. Harry, in the words of his colleagues, is the greatest, the best in his business, the business of surveillance or scoptophilia. At the time this film was released in 1974, the nation was still saturated with the sequelae of Watergate. Electronic surveillance and concomitant concerns over issues of privacy and confidentiality were the focus of media attention. (Managed care, and the Patriot Act, had not yet desensitized us to the dissolution of confidentiality.) Harry's visible caul is his raincoat. It is a membrane that is translucent and distorts what it covers, like so many other surfaces in the film. This creates a visual ambiguity to parallel and support the auditory ambiguity that is the subject of the film. The central irony is that the more sophisticated and precise the technology by which sounds can be recorded, preserved, and retrieved, the greater the difficulty in discovering their meaning. ". . . Empty eyeballs knew / That knowledge increases unreality, that / Mirror on mirror mirrored is all the show" (Yeats, 1983b, pp. 336–337).

Harry, whose only concern is the quality of the sound, totally misinterprets it when he becomes interested in its meaning. But his misinterpretation makes psychodynamic sense. His single-minded focus on the technology serves to obscure from himself the unconscious motivation for his spying on others. He denies that there is anything personal or of value in his apartment, yet it is all locked up—a representation of his psyche. He is completely defended, yet feels there is nothing to defend or defend against. There is an evisceration of meaning, a denial that meaning exists. The only way in which he can pursue his fanatical and compulsive voyeurism is to persuade himself that he is not interested in what he perceives. This schism between perception and meaning has become progressively wider in our culture over the past few decades. We consume more percepts than ever before and are ever more oblivious of their meaning. The 1970s, when this film was made, was a decade influenced by Marshall McLuhan's slogan, "The medium is the message" (1964), a rationale for the hybrid form known as "infotainment" which so dominates our current media.

Despite his most strenuous efforts to conceal his secrets, Harry reveals them. First, we become aware that all of his locks have not kept the landlady from leaving a birthday present in his apartment. As he protests to her that he has nothing personal, he is taking off his pants. Earlier, the sinister and mocking behavior of the mime in Union Square Park also suggests that Harry is not anonymous. Next, we hear his girlfriend, Amy, singing "Red Red Robin," the same song sung by the female conspirator he has been watching. In church, he confesses to superficial sins while thinking about a more serious sin: collecting evidence that he thinks will be used to "hurt two young people." This covers a more basic, unconscious sin (childhood wish), to possess his mother and do away with his father.

Harry allows the people from the surveillance convention into his most protected space, his holy of holies, where his secrets are kept. He also allows Moran to plant a bug (pen) on him. When Martin Stett, the director's assistant, tells him he is being watched, he does not change his residence or quit the director's employ. Likewise, at the end of the film when he discovers that his apartment is bugged, he compulsively searches for the bug rather than move out. He is a technologist to the bitter end, fixated on the method to the fatal omission of the meaning.

This oedipal tale is post Watergate and post Kafka. It is clear by the middle of the film, the episode in which Stett tells him that he is being watched, that the subject of the surveillance is Harry Caul. If they can watch him, the watcher, without his being aware of it, why did they need him to watch the young couple? Obviously, they did not. Their retaining him, therefore, was a test of him and the conspiracy is merely a way of involving him. Indeed, it is ultimately unclear whether the conspiracy in either of its versions is not Harry's fantasy. The first version of the fantasy is an Othello theme in which a close lieutenant of the general's undermines his trust in his woman and provokes him to a fit of murderous jealousy. In this case, however, the jealousy leads him into a premeditated trap in which he is murdered.

Harry is privy to all the variations of this fantasy and their respective outcomes because his patterns of impulse, guilt, and identification have given rise to all of them. Witness the fact that the murderer is dressed in a translucent plastic garment and the dead man is also wrapped in plastic. Harry's caul covers these people because, by identification, they are Harry. Further, the fact that all of them are wrapped in plastic becomes a symbol for the distinctively modern and postmodern way to sanitize and cosmetize things that are ugly, repugnant, sinful, and natural: for example, the way raw meat and poultry are wrapped in supermarkets, the way a baby's feces and urine are contained in plastic diapers; even body bags are plastic. Plastic lets you dissociate: you can see the horror without having to smell it. It keeps consequences at bay. "He's not hurting anyone. Neither are we." When you obliterate the boundary between reality and illusion, you can always pretend that you have not hurt anyone.

In exploiting the symbolic potential of plastic, perhaps Coppola was consciously or unconsciously recalling another film conversation, the one that takes place in *The Graduate* (Nichols, 1967), in which one of the guests at his graduation party advises the title character, played by Dustin Hoffman, to go into the plastics business. Here, again, the context is cheating and deception.

In the first scene of *The Conversation*, the long-range microphone in the window resembles a sniper's rifle. This underscores the link between perceptual penetration of another's boundaries and assassination. Harry's work in New York led to three people being murdered. When reminded of this, his conscience begins to overwhelm him.

There is a sign in the loft where Harry's shop is located that reads, "Smoking." Clearly, the word "No" has been excised. In the id, "No" does not exist. The implication is that prohibitions and inhibitions are cast aside under the pressure to obtain forbidden knowledge. But the absence of "No" also suggests castration. Castration is implied, too, by the presence of the Doberman that comes into the director's office when Harry enters it. Another irony reflected by this setting is the sign, "Private," on the door, despite the fact that the tapes can be heard clearly by anyone in the corridor. Obviously, there is no privacy.

Harry's curiosity seems to be focused on—nay, riveted on—the things that are lost or obscured from his perception. What was said or done during the interval when the couple under surveillance are blocked from view? When the lights go out on the bus, Harry is reminded of that gap, that moment of lost contact. What does it recall from his childhood? What do parents do together when you are not watching them? What happens to mother when you cannot see her? What happens to you? What is the significance of finding nothing where you expect something to be?

That Harry, at times, entertains homosexual fantasies in order to assuage such fears is suggested in the party scene where he cuts in on a dancing couple and, apparently facetiously, begins to dance with the man, who happens to be a police officer carrying a pistol in an ostentatiously displayed shoulder holster. Apropos Harry's fascination with gaps, we should recall the famous seventeen-second gap in the Nixon tapes. Nature may abhor a vacuum, but they intrigue. The only personal expression Harry allows himself is playing the saxophone to a minus-one record, the sound of a band with one instrument missing. He fills the gap, but he does so in an empty apartment with an imaginary audience. To Amy, his abandoned girlfriend, he describes himself as a freelance musician.

In the end, I suppose there is a coherence and significance to the film. The performances are believable and the camera and sound work are appropriate to the theme. My objection is that it is too self-consciously symbolic and "Freudian." It is the kind of film psychoanalysts like because they can analyze it. Like a good patient, it is analyzable. But this is an insufficient criterion for judging a work of art. It also makes life too easy for the analyst, who should learn to work with materials that are less tailor-made.

I prefer works—novels, films, plays—in which the author's intention is to create a simulacrum of her experience in as truthful a way as she can and allow the symbols (if there are any) to emerge of their own accord. If the work is wrought with skill, knowledge, and passion, I believe that this will happen as a matter of course. When we, the audience, engage with such a work, the symbols will appear to us as intrinsic, and inextricable from its texture rather than super-imposed or contrived.

The Sopranos: Gangsta angst

The series to which the two episodes, "Big Girls Don't Cry" and "D Girl" (Chase, 2000), belong is called *The Sopranos* because it is about singing. There are three meanings to the term *family* as it applies to *The Sopranos*. These are conveniently seen as arranged in concentric circles with Tony Soprano at the center. The most proximal circle consists of his blood relatives, nuclear and extended; the second, of his criminal organization; the third, of all the additional characters who regularly appear in the episodes. Chief among the latter is, of course, Dr. Melfi, Tony's psychiatrist. I might even be tempted to include a fourth circle at the periphery of the configuration, by far the most populous. It would encompass all the viewers who owe such a deal of voyeuristic and identificatory gratification to the occupants of the inner circles.

In a very important sense, then, we are all sopranos, for if we do not ourselves sing, we certainly make use of others to do our singing for us. Because this is a story about an Italian family, the singing must bear some relation to the tradition of opera, Neapolitan street singing, the *bel canto* style, and the transplanted derivatives in the singing of several generations of Italian American pop balladeers. The subjects of this singing are family ties, love, betrayal, revenge, violence, remorse, guilt, and shame.

Now, there is a special underworld connotation to the word *sing*: It implies confession, usually with the intention of incriminating one's associates. In *The Sopranos*, however, this intention is far less often the motive for the singing than the almost universal need to share one's secrets with at least one other person, and sometimes a great many more than that. Thus, we have Chris obsessed with telling his story to movie audiences, Carmela confiding in Father Phil, Uncle Junior entrusting his lady friends with intimate secrets, Paulie seeing a shrink, Pussy singing to the FBI, and the nodal self-disclosure of Tony to Dr. Melfi. If these were not sufficient, the recipients of the confessions must consult confessors of their own: Dr. Melfi sees her supervisor/therapist, Dr. Elliot Kupferberg, and the two of them con-sult, together, with a third supervisor at especially difficult moments.

It is the ubiquity of the impulse to share secrets that makes the theme of betrayal a component of the very air these characters breathe. We, in the fourth circle, ironically, are privy to all the secrets; we are the unseen viewers regarding whom Count Guido da Montefeltro, an inhabitant of the Hell imagined and depicted by another famous Italian—the poet, Dante—says, "If I thought my reply were to some-one who could ever return to the world, this flame would waver no more, but since, I'm told nobody ever escapes from this pit, I'll tell you [my story] without fear of infamy" (Alighieri, 1951, p. 204). The count is addressing Dante, who is only visiting Hell and will, indeed, return to the world above with the express intention of telling the very story that the speaker hesitates to share from fear of being defamed. And we, the audience, like Dante, and unlike most of the characters in *The Sopranos*, are under no obligation to hold what we have learned in confidence.

My plan is to discuss a number of the major themes reflected in the two episodes as they bear on the therapeutic situation involving Tony and Dr. Melfi. The themes fall roughly under the rubrics of psychic determinism as opposed to the possibility of personality change; the mutual influences of gangster movies and gangster behavior; the nature of the songs sung by the Sopranos; and the engagement of experience with innocence.

* * *

When Dr. Melfi meets with her supervisor/therapist, Elliot, in the episode named "Big Girls Don't Cry," she describes a dream in which Tony suffers a panic attack behind the wheel of his car and, as a result, crashes into a truck. In the background, she hears a song from the film, *The Wizard of Oz* (Fleming & Cukor, 1939). To Elliot's query about which character in the movie reminds her of Tony, she acknowledges that she associates Tony with the Great Oz, himself, whom she charac-terizes as a powerful, dominant male. In fact, the eponymous wizard turned out to be an impotent, bemused man behind all the machinery of illusion, but she does not seem to recall this, and Elliot, whether from ignorance or tact, fails to remind her. But there is the implication that a significant discrepancy exists between Melfi's conscious view of Tony's power and her unconscious grasp of his relative helplessness to control the array of internal and external forces that impinge on him.

The episode opens with Adriana, Chris's girlfriend, cautioning him against being late to his "first session"; she adds, "If you're late, they won't refund my money." Although Chris is on his way to an acting class, her calling it a session and emphasizing his financial responsibility are more typical of the conventions of psychotherapy and serve to establish a parallel between Tony's psychiatric treatment and the later effects of the acting class on Chris's psyche—most pointedly, his inability to play the gentleman caller in *The Glass Menagerie*. Instead, he chooses to act the rebel without a cause, a role that fits him all to well, as he learns, to his distress. The message seems to be that the past is an inescapable template that determines later behavior and that any attempt to alter its effects are doomed to failure.

During the period after which Dr. Melfi has terminated Tony's treatment, Tony feels a powerful need to speak with someone in a quasi-therapeutic role. He turns to Hesh, the advisor and wise man, but the results are mixed. Hesh seems unable or unwilling to become the recipient of Tony's anxiety and depression, deflecting it with platitudes or countering it with descriptions of his own medical problems. In the end, however, he surprises Tony with the disclosure that Tony's father had had experiences that were remarkably similar to Tony's panic attacks. He also mentions having heard of an MRI procedure that can detect brain activity indicative of a fear response to parental criticism, a fact that has implications for Tony's relation to his mother.

The resumption of Tony's treatment with Dr. Melfi is the outcome of a remarkable sequence of events. First, Melfi bursts into a rage at Elliot when he suggests that her reason for wishing to treat Tony again is that, "Treating a mobster provides you with a vicarious thrill." She bolts from the office, shouting, "You smug cocksucker: fuck you!" Her tantrum is uncharacteristic of the usually composed, articulate, and sensitive psychiatrist. In fact, it is as atypical of her as it is typical of her favorite patient, leading us to the inescapable conclusion that she is unconsciously identified with him. To those familiar with Freud's formulation that loss can cause the shadow of the object to fall upon the ego, this should come as no surprise, even if the loss is temporary. That this has occurred at all is a measure of Tony's importance to Dr. Melfi.

Parallel to Dr. Melfi's loss of self-control, we find Tony increasingly unable to prevent himself from losing it. In the scene immediately following Melfi's blow-up, Tony responds to learning that his sister has taken a second mortgage on their mother's house by smashing a telephone with Carmela and Tony Jr. looking on. After the mandatory moment of bravado, he appears deeply ashamed and upset with himself, apologizing to Carmela and attempting to square things with A. J. by making a lame joke.

Later in the episode, presumably recovered from her outburst, Melfi returns to Elliot's office. This time, her identification with Tony is manifested in her overeating and consequent weight gain. Persisting in her belief that she has abandoned Tony and, therefore, must offer to resume treating him, draws a singularly unpsychodynamic reply from Dr. Kupferberg: he warns her to restrict her use of sugar and artificial sweeteners. Is this a thinly disguised reference to her excessive drinking? Or is it a covert admonition to her to avoid sentimentalized and Pollyanna-like rationalizations for seeing Tony again? In the last exchange of the session, she denies feeling sexually attracted to Tony but adds, "He can be such a little boy sometimes," evidence, perhaps, of maternal feelings that ward off an underlying sexual attraction and a wish to castrate Tony or cut him down to size.

These inferences receive support from the scene that follows. The phone call in which she invites Tony to resume his treatment is made from her home rather than her office and she has fortified herself for it by drinking wine. She reaches Tony in his car, where he is awaiting the return of Furio, who has been engaged in enforcement with the proprietors of a brothel. Melfi's language is especially pertinent: after urging him to resume therapy, she says, "If you want, I could fit you in tomorrow at 2:30," and then asks, "So, do I put you down?" Sufficiently disinhibited by the alcohol, she uses imagery that conveys, unmistakably, her unconscious intent: to "fit" Tony in, which condenses sexuality and maternity; to "put [Tony] down" carries a range of connotations, including to denigrate him, to put him to sleep, and to kill him. Tony's response is, "Nah, fuck it." Melfi asks, "Why do you say that?" Tony answers dismissively before Furio's arrival makes it necessary that he cut the connection.

Predictably, however, the next scene finds Tony in Melfi's office. Melfi is visibly pleased to a degree that conveys how radically she has deviated from any semblance of analytic neutrality. Against the advice of her therapist/supervisor, she has acted upon her impulsive need to resume the relationship with Tony and seems to find the experience intensely pleasurable. Tony, in contrast, appears distinctly uncomfortable. He rolls his head and sits with his legs apart in an attitude that is at once routinely macho and almost impotently vulnerable. Melfi begins by treating him as a little boy: "Still taking your medications?" she asks. When he responds equivocally, she assumes a doctorly tone, instructing him to "Take it or don't take it" but then adding, "Okay?" in a voice that is more conciliatory, less parental, and even a little submissive. She goes on to press her advantage, however, by referring to his panic attack and the auto accident it had caused, the counterpart and instigation of her dream. He denies its importance, treating it as ancient history.

At this point, Tony's body language becomes eloquent: he reaches laboriously down to bring his ankle over his knee, covering his vulnerable genitals. This gesture precedes his sharing what he learned from Hesh, that there is a history of panic attacks in his family and that his father had them. His manner in conveying this intelligence is smug and triumphant, as though it were an iron-clad refutation of all of Melfi's psychogenic assumptions about him. (For example, in one of the episodes of the first season, Dr. Melfi indicated to Tony that biology is not destiny and Anthony Jr. is not doomed to live the wiseguy life style of Tony and his grandfather.) He is relieved by the possibility that the roots of his problem are organic and genetic because this absolves him from personal responsibility and the necessity to struggle with his inner demons.

Here, Dr. Melfi asks Tony what he wants to achieve. "What I want to achieve!" he snaps, "I want to stop passing out; I want to stop fucking panicking; I want to direct my power and my fucking anger against the people in my life that deserve it. I want to be in total control," as though completely negating the comforting assertion he has just made that his problems are biologically determined. Melfi counters, "There's no such thing as total control." "Of course there is," says Tony. With some heat, Melfi replies, "You want to be a better gang leader, read *The Art of War* by Sun Tzu" (2001).

This provokes Tony to declare, angrily, "You know what? Fuck you! You know who I am; you know what I do. You called me! You know where I was yesterday when you called? I was outside a whorehouse while a guy who works for me was inside, beating the shit out of a guy that owes me money—broke his arm, put a bullet in his kneecap."

"How'd that make you feel?" asks Melfi. "Wished it was me in there," answers Tony. "Giving the beating or taking it?" is the psychiatrist's riposte.

Thus, in a short, highly charged exchange, the theme of freedom of the will *vs.* determinism is repeated in an intriguing set of variations by the two virtuoso singers. Tony introduces biological necessity. Melfi parries by asking what he wishes to achieve in treatment, a question that presupposes the possibility of change. Tony's response betrays a tacit acceptance of the possibility of change and its correlate, responsibility. Melfi rejects Tony's treatment goal of becoming a better gang leader as inappropriate. Tony reverts to a less categorical version of his deterministic position, reminds Melfi that the treatment has been resumed at her instigation, and attempts to make a mockery of her hopes for his changing through self-understanding by describing the brutal situation in which he took her phone call of reconciliation. The duet ends with Melfi's ominous and ambiguous question, "Giving the beating or taking it?" and its evocation of the helpless need to identify with a powerful aggressor in order to avoid being victimized. The only consistency in this material is the consistency of character— *la raison que raison ne connais pas* (Pascal, 2009, p. 5): the rationale that cannot be comprehended by reason, which is only intelligible in what Yeats has called "The foul rag and bone shop of the heart" (1983c, pp. 346–348).

In the episode's final scene, Chris is seen collecting the hard copies, the discs, and all the other records of his autobiographical script, to throw them in the dumpster. His chances of change and redemption through art are over: he has tried other roles; it has not worked.

* * *

If you think these issues have been laid to rest, however, you do not know *The Sopranos.* The very next episode opens with an event involving Anthony Jr., whose experiences will again confront Tony with questions of choice and necessity. And, lest we forget Chris, we learn, a few minutes into the episode, that Adriana has rescued a copy of his script from oblivion. It is clear, then, that stories cannot be suppressed, songs cannot be silenced, and conflicts can never be permanently resolved.

Carmela and Tony demand from Anthony Jr. an explanation of his behavior in appropriating and damaging Carmela's car. What they get for their pains is a dose of existential despair. A. J., in a classic *non sequitur* to his father's cruel broaching of his bed-wetting in summer camp, says, "Death just shows the ultimate absurdity of life." Outraged, Tony thunders, "What is this? Are you trying to get me to lose my temper? Because I'm about to put you through that Goddam window!" A. J. quietly remarks, "There is no God." Here, Meadow arrives to assuage her parents' consternation by explaining that A. J.'s English teacher has assigned him Camus's *The Stranger*, a novel about a man who seems unmoved by the death of his mother. A. J. asks, "Do you ever think, 'Why were we born?'" Meadow puts in, "Madame deStael says that in life we must choose between boredom and suffering." Anthony Jr. is prey to both. He is the stranger in his family because, unlike his father, whose symptoms are discussed in the privacy of a psychiatrist's office, his are used to shame him publicly.

Two scenes later, Tony describes the incident to Dr. Melfi as follows: Anthony Jr. asks why he was born if God does not exist. Tony tells his son that *his* existence has cost him a lot of money and, if Anthony feels his life is valueless, he wants his money back. Dr. Melfi then asks whether Tony is vexed with his son because he damaged Carmela's car. Tony denies this is the reason for his irritation, citing, instead, Anthony's nihilism and despair. Melfi assures him that this type of anxiety is typical of adolescence, and asks whether Tony ever experienced it. Tony replies that his own parents would never have tolerated it.

This reference to Tony's parents provides an opening for Dr. Melfi to ask after Tony's mother. Tony says that she is dead to him. Melfi asks how that has affected Anthony, and whether Tony is able to explain to Anthony his estrangement from his mother and the resulting stressful family ambience. Tony asserts that the situation in his family is no justification for Anthony's disrespectful attitude.

Melfi ventures that Anthony has discovered existentialism. Bemused, Tony assumes that Anthony is unduly influenced by the internet. Melfi enlightens him by explaining that, as a result of the mind-numbing events of the Second World War, existentialism posited that there are no eternal verities and promoted a comprehensive questioning of meaning and reality. Tony asks whether Dr. Melfi subscribes to this. She counters by stating that, indeed, the very institution of motherhood is compromised in Tony's own family. Tony protests that he insists that Anthony show the proper filial attitudes and behavior to Carmela.

Dr. Melfi parries by confronting him about his own mother's murderous betrayal of him. Tony tries to shrug this off by saying that the discussion of his mother is unnecessary since he now entertains no illusions about her intentions. Melfi asks whether Anthony is aware of Tony's declaration that he regards his mother as dead. Tony says he does not know. Melfi wonders whether, if Anthony had heard this from his father, it might contribute to his sense of futility and despair.

Tony becomes defensive, assuming that Melfi is blaming him for Anthony's problem. Assuring him that she is not, she adds that the dawning realization that the ultimate responsibility for one's choices, behavior, and construction of experience, lies with oneself, and that endings (separation and loss) are inevitable, might produce a profound sense of unease, a malignant belief that the only dependable reality is death.

With a sudden flash of respect, Tony tells Dr. Melfi that he thinks Anthony may have a valid point.

I have paraphrased this long dialogue because I believe it explicates and elaborates a critical experience for Tony as well as for many of the other characters. It also illustrates the way in which Tony's therapy plies the interface of psychology and morality. This is, in part, because to treat Tony at all, Dr. Melfi must struggle with whether it is moral and ethical to work with an avowed criminal and, if so, whether her work can circumvent the reprehensible character of much of his behavior. Further, the scene is a counterpoint to the one in the previous episode in which the theme of psychic determinism first comes under direct scrutiny. If Tony had the total control over his own behavior to which he aspires, he would, thereby, be totally responsible for his actions, and, therefore, accountable for them. If he is nothing more than the agent of his biological programming, he cannot be held responsible for his actions.

There is an intrinsic relationship between the need to sing (tell one's own story; partake in psychotherapy) and the suffering that results from a sense of one's own powerlessness. The more worldly power he gains and exercises, the more aware Tony becomes of his lack of power over himself and, hence, the more he has to sing. His powerlessness over himself is symbolized by his psychiatric symptoms—chiefly his panic attacks. It is ironic that the behavior he has asked Dr. Melfi to relieve him of is precisely that which rescues him from being an unmitigated character disorder, bereft of a humanity capable of redemption and without a motive for self-observation. Dr. Melfi's explication of the existential predicament affects Tony with a shock of recognition. For the first time, perhaps, he grasps that what lies at the heart of his symptoms is the intense dread that results from an acknowledgement of personal responsibility, the chill, aching anger that cannot be given direct expression.

*   *   *

The episode called "D Girl" is an exploration of the mutual influences of gangster movies and gangsters. Especially apropos is a recent newspaper account (*New York Daily News*, 2015), of the funeral, in Rome, of an important Mafia don. The musical accompaniment to the cortege was the theme from Coppola's *The Godfather* (1972). The interlude elaborates on the events of Chris's abortive forays into the world of make-believe. What is symbolized in his first aspirations to become a screen writer is, as I have previously hinted, his need to sing (tell his story), as well as a sketchily conceived hope of trading up from his position as a low-level hoodlum to the glamour and comparative respectability of show business, That is, he wants to assume a primary and creative role. Complementary to the allure that the movies hold for Chris is the fascination of filmmakers and their audiences with organized crime.

As dramatized in Chris's acting classes, he is experiencing considerable dis-ease related to unconscious unresolved conflicts involving his father. This results in a periodic eruption of transferential ambivalence to Tony. The oedipal nature of his feelings is reflected in his questioning Tony's leadership as well as his drifting away from the mafia crew and towards the film enterprise. Ami, the "D Girl" of the title, is successful in seducing Chris literally and figuratively, so that she can steal the parts of his script that will lend verisimilitude to the one that she and her boss, Jon, are developing. On his side, Chris allows himself to believe that his special criminal aura will suffice to induce the film people to help him to perfect his script and accept him into their world. Art and life interpenetrate in the hotel room scene where Jon and Chris titillate each other with glimpses of each other's worlds, and Jon suggests a plot twist in which the protagonist of Chris's script murders his own father. This excites Chris because it constitutes a fantasied resolution of his oedipal conflict.

In other episodes, we have been shown how the gangsters are attracted to films depicting criminals. Silvio, for example, rehearses, *ad nauseam*, Edward G. Robinson's "Is this the end of Rico?" speech from *Little Caesar* (LeRoy, 1931). The scene in Chris's first acting class ends with Chris glancing to his left, as though his attention were diverted to something peripheral. What he seems to see is a television set tuned to the nightly news, but the set is located in Tony's living room, Chris's glance serving as a transitional device. This segue highlights the connection between Chris's involvement in the media and Tony's, because the subject of the clip being televised is a federal investigation of the Soprano crime family. Tony takes umbrage at the undesirable publicity; he does his singing in the privacy of Dr. Melfi's office. Chris would like to do his before the cameras.

Of course, the cross-fertilization of the Cosa Nostra and the film industry is best exemplified in precisely such a series as *The Sopranos*, the influence of which is certain to perpetuate this peculiarly reverberating circuit, just as the *Godfather* (1972), *Miller's Crossing* (Coen & Coen, 1990), *Goodfellas* (Scorsese, 1990), and many of their precursors did. We, the audience, are susceptible to the same scoptophilic impulse attributed to Dr. Melfi by Dr. Kupferberg. When he asks her why we love roller coasters and scary movies, she replies, "To experience the thrill of being terrified without the consequences." Like Tony, we prefer to eschew the responsibility, if not for our actions, at least for our impulses. Our voyeurism resembles that of Jon Favreau, his assistant, Ami, and David Chase, who created *The Sopranos* to pander to our insatiable curiosity about behavior that we regard as evil. The dissolution of the boundaries between gangster life and art took on a new and bizarre aspect when Robert Iler, the young actor who portrays Anthony Jr., was arrested for participating in an actual robbery.

The final sequence of the "D Girl" episode focuses on Christopher's return to the family following his cinematic detour, his dream of successful rebellion against his destiny ended. As he sits on the steps of the Soprano home meditating on Tony's ultimatum, the soundtrack consists of the voice of an actual soprano singing a quasi-operatic aria. Against this background, Chris returns to the house, submitting to the unalterable law of his history, and suppressing, at least for the moment, his oedipal competitiveness with Tony.

The Sopranos sing for the same reasons we all sing, because we suffer and our suffering is relieved when we tell stories. The prototype of this need is Coleridge's *Ancient Mariner* (1968), who, from inner compulsion, must repeat his story to an endless succession of listeners. Presumably, were we to find the ideal listener, one who could effect the "psychodialysis" that would detoxify our narratives, we would be freed to develop new and divergent tales. This is Tony's unconscious hope. It is expressed in his many fantasies about innocence, such as the one evoked in him by the family of ducks that, for a while, make his swimming pool their home, as well as by the figure of the happy wanderer in the episode between the two I have been discussing. Flight is the expedient that distinguishes these innocents; their freedom, in this respect, provokes Tony's envy. They can escape from their formative environment into a new element, taking their families with them and leaving all the poisonous influences behind.

*   *   *

The Sopranos is an extraordinary series that ushered in a new era for television, one in which well wrought dramatic works, pitched to intelligent and sophisticated audiences, could be presented over extended time periods. How the collective efforts of so many collaborators could result in so cohesive and richly nuanced a product is a question that others may explore. The intention of the present chapter was nothing more than to attempt an interpretation that demonstrates the inherent depth of the material.

CHAPTER TWO

Time and death

"Depend on it, sir, when a man knows he is to be hanged in a fortnight, it concentrates his mind wonderfully." The quotation is from Samuel Johnson, *The Life of Samuel Johnson LL.D. Vol. 3* (Boswell, 1872, p. 167). It underscores the urgency and highly charged tone of human behavior under the acute awareness of imminent endings. It is this atmosphere that is breathed by the characters in *Dr. Strangelove* (Kubrick, 1964), *Up in the Air* (Reitman, 2009), and *Tunes of Glory* (Kennaway, 1956).

A remarkable phenomenon depicted in *Dr. Strangelove* is the repression and suppression of consequences by the major characters. Their actions have led to the inevitable destruction of the world, yet they behave as though their lives will go on. The character of Dr. Strangelove, himself, epitomizes this almost casual evasion of awareness. In the face of nuclear holocaust, he assumes the perspective of a cheerful futurologist whose vision is fixed on the situation that will follow the end. He shares this proclivity with all fundamentalists who so easily renounce the manifest world for a place in the next one: eschatology is the province of the damning and the damned.

Ryan Bingham, the protagonist of *Up in the Air*, specializes in awakening people to the finitude of their lives. His problem, as dramatized in the film, is that he has focused so exclusively on endings that he has totally neglected the events that precede them. Chief among these are human relationships, the emotions that make them necessary, and those that they inspire. If the people he serves have repressed death and endings, he has repressed life, and the experiences of which it is made.

Tunes of Glory is a study of soldiers, men for whom sudden, violent death is a ubiquitous event in wartime, and a haunting presence at all times. To metabolize this experience is exceedingly difficult and fraught with innumerable daunting complexities, as is becoming increasingly and painfully clear from the testimony of veterans of the several Middle Eastern conflicts. The ways in which these men defend against the psychic impact of the particular devastation to which they have been exposed are examined in the film.

In the essay in Chapter One on *Notes on a Scandal,* I explore two ways of looking at time used by the ancient Greeks: *chronos,* ordinary sequential time, and *kairos,* rare moments when time appears to be suspended. These ideas are especially relevant to *Dr. Strangelove, Up in the Air,* and *Tunes of Glory,* the three films I shall discuss under the category of time and death. The atmosphere of urgency, and the imminence of endings often transfigure events and render them kaironic. Film-makers are acutely attuned to this effect and design their imagery to reflect and dramatize the contrast between the two modes of experiencing time.

Dr. Strangelove: Let's get this over with

First, a little background. The film was made in 1964; the Cold War had begun in 1947; the Bay of Pigs fiasco took place in 1961; the Berlin Wall was also built in 1961; the Cuban Missile Crisis occurred in 1962; John F. Kennedy was assassinated in 1963. The novel from which the film was developed was written by Peter George, an Englishman, who published it in the UK under the pseudonym, Peter Bryant. The novel was called *Two Hours to Doom* (Bryant, 1958). It was later published in the United States, under his own name, with the title *Red Alert* (George, 1958). The film was made in England.

Its satirical intent is immediately conveyed in the initial disclaimer that, "It is the stated policy of the United States Air Force that their safeguards would prevent the occurrence of such events as are depicted in the film." The emphasis, of course, is on the word *stated*, implying that there might be discrepancies between what is stated, what is intended, and, indeed, what is possible—suppositions that are strongly supported by the film itself.

Briefly, the film is set in three locales: the interior of the B-52 bomber, Burpelson Air Force Base, and the Pentagon's War Room, with momentary cuts to a mid-air refueling, General Turgidson's hotel suite, the cloud-shrouded landscape of the opening credits, and the choreographed nuclear explosions of the final sequence.

The characters include the crew of the B-52, a parody of the military groupings to be found in all the propagandistic Second World War films, consisting of at least one representative of each major ethnic minority, in this case, a black (James Earl Jones in one of his earliest roles), a Jew, and several less easily identifiable types. The leader, quite appropriately, is a Texan, Major T. T. "King" Kong, played by Slim Pickens, in a masterpiece of casting. The principal figures at Burpelson Air Force Base are General Jack D. Ripper, (Sterling Hayden), Group Captain Lionel Mandrake (Peter Sellers in one of his three roles), and Colonel Bat Guano, played by Keenan Wynn. In the Pentagon's War Room, we find president Merkin Muffley (Sellers, again), General Buck Turgidson, (George C. Scott), Soviet Ambassador Desadeski (Peter Bull), Dr. Strangelove (Sellers, yet again), and a largely faceless group of presidential advisors.

The plot is simple: Ripper gives the attack order, Mandrake tries to stop it; they do not succeed; the doomsday machine is revealed and activated; the mine shaft plan is introduced; the world is destroyed.

The film is a satire. That is, it attempts to expose folly and vice by using ridicule, sarcasm, irony, and contempt. Its basic objectives are to teach and amuse. Dare I say it, the thrust of this film is to demonstrate how some of the most cherished values, assumptions, and institutions of American civilization, taken to their extreme, could result in world destruction. Since the tendencies that the film examines most closely are derivatives of crass sexuality and aggression, a psychoanalytic interpretation is highly appropriate.

*   *   *

Let's go back to the characters. Each is named for the quality that most typifies him. (Note that I am not using the masculine pronoun here out of ignorance of what is politically correct, but because there is literally only one female role in the film, a very minor one. This is highly significant and I shall have more to say about it later.)

Take, for example, Jack D. Ripper. We are all familiar with the serial butchery of prostitutes in Victorian London committed by a person who was dubbed Jack the Ripper by the contemporary press. Ripper, then is a symbol of singular viciousness directed against women.

Both of Lionel Mandrake's names are meaningful. The name Lionel is a diminutive of the word lion. The lion is a symbol of Great Britain and its once proud empire, now so diminished in size and strength as to be a Lionel. A mandrake is a plant root that is said to have the appearance of a small man; it is used as an herbal remedy for impotence or lack of virility. Thus, the Group Captain is a little man as well as a small lion, but he does retain some potency, in contrast to his commander, General Ripper.

Speaking of generals, Buck is the epithet applied to a virile male animal, and Turgid signifies swollen or tumescent, as an erect penis. Perhaps the patronymic form is used to suggest that though the General is the issue of a turgid penis, his own may not be.

The president's name, Merkin Muffley, is interesting not merely because of its denotation but also because it seems to betray a quality sometimes discerned by critics in the work of Stanley Kubrick— namely, misogyny. Merkin is British slang for the female pubic area, and Muffley is a word for a pubic-hair wig.

The Russian ambassador is called Desadeski which, when we remove the Slavic suffix, becomes deSade, elsewhere known as "The Divine Marquis," the eighteenth-century French nobleman whose name has become synonymous with deliberate destructiveness, in general, and with the derivation of pleasure from sexual violence, especially when inflicted on women.

Major "King" Kong is named for the huge ape of the eponymous film (Cooper & Schoedsack, 1933) (much beloved of Fay Wray), who wreaked havoc on the civilized world when goaded by humans. Guano, as we know, is the excrement of flying creatures, so that Colonel Bat Guano is equated with the unloading of deleterious or destructive materials from on high, a prototype, perhaps, of the SAC bombers and their deadly cargo.

Late in the film, we learn that Dr. Strangelove's German name was Merkwuerdigichliebe, literally translated as Strangelove, which might have been a more felicitous choice for the section of the *DSM IV* (American Psychiatric Association, 1994, pp. 522–532) that goes under the rubric of paraphilias. Those who still remember the *DSM III* (American Psychiatric Association, 1980) would have known it as "sexual deviations."

Then there is the assortment of minor names: Dmitri Kissof, for the off-screen character of the Russian premier, a symbol of dismissiveness, deflection of responsibility, and rejection; Burpelson Air Force Base, named no doubt, in honor of a distinguished air hero associated with the oral expulsion of air consequent to the digestive process; and the Bland Corporation, a transparent reference to the infamous Rand Corporation, the highest-powered military consulting firm in the nation, from which little has been heard since the Vietnam War.

* * *

A principal target of Kubrick's attack on American institutions is the phallic–narcissistic character type that has attained the status of the ideal towards which all males in our culture should strive. In the film, it is represented by Generals Turgidson and Ripper, Colonel Guano, Major Kong, and, in a more complex way, by Captain Mandrake and Dr. Strangelove. We must begin with the observation that machines rather than people accomplish the only sexual consummation in the film. Indeed, the film opens with a shot of copulating airplanes and closes with nuclear orgasms. But it is significant that Buck Turgidson's liaison with Miss Scot, the only female character in the film, is interrupted by the call that informs Turgidson of the emergency, and that liaison is never to be resumed. Speaking to her on the phone from the War Room, Turgidson explains, "I can't talk to you now, my president needs me," emphasizing the power of patriarchy over heterosexual eros in a society dominated by the phallic–narcissistic principle; he also consoles her with the lines, "I know how it is, baby. Tell you what you do. You just start your countdown and old Bucky will be back here before you can say, 'Blast off'," his imagery betraying the pervasive tendency to translate human sexual functions into those of engines of destruction.

The gynophobic theme that is so central to the film receives its strongest representation in the character of General Ripper. Indeed, it would not overstate the case to say that the entire inciting event of the story—the irrevocable dispatching of the nuclear bombers to their targets—is the result of Ripper's fear of women. Describing the origins of his belief that the fluoridation of drinking water is a communist plot to contaminate "precious bodily fluids," he confides to Mandrake,

> I first became aware of it during the physical act of love ... Yes a profound sense of fatigue, a feeling of emptiness, followed. Luckily I was able to interpret these feelings correctly: loss of Essence ... I can assure you it has not recurred, Mandrake.

> Women ... women sense my power, and they seek the life essence. I do not avoid women, Mandrake, but I do deny them my essence.

He believes that drinking water that has been contaminated by fluoridation metabolizes into products that taint body fluids by diminishing their vigor and potency; his psychotic thinking then links this diminution with his post coital languor.

Next, having presumably remedied the problem by abstemiously avoiding ordinary drinking water, he betrays the unconscious fantasy that is its actual cause by adding that he denies women his essence. So, it is not sufficient to restore the purity of his semen; he must also take the further step of withholding it from women. Clearly, then, the real enemy, at an unconscious level, is the woman, whose objective, he feels, is to weaken and deplete him. Unable to accept this view of women at a conscious level, he projects it as an international communist conspiracy. Of course, the infantile prototype that is so distortedly reflected in Ripper's aquaphobia is mother's milk and the process of nursing, with all of its implications for weakness, helplessness, and dependency. The General's fear and hatred of this powerful maternal figure results in unrelenting envy and greed that he projects onto women, seeing them as intent on stealing and marauding his precious contents, and leaving him depleted. But, since motherhood is an institution sacred to the macho American hero, the onus cannot remain with women; it must be displaced onto the evil empire. One consequence of this displacement is that the sadistic impulses attributed to the enemy assume a homosexual character. When convinced that he is shortly to be captured by the troops attacking the air force base, he imagines he will be tortured until he reveals the recall code. Rather than submit, he commits suicide. The torture, in his fantasies, would no doubt take the form of homosexual rape, corresponding to the unrequited, disavowed, and, therefore, undiminished, wish for oral gratification. Additional evidence for his latent homosexual impulses, and their origins in oral longing, can be found in Mandrake's words when attempting to humor him into cooperation, "And if those devils come back and try any rough stuff, we'll fight them together, boy, like we did just now, on the floor, eh? You with the old gun and me with the belt and ammo, feeding you, Jack! 'Feed me,' you said, and I was feeding you, Jack."

* * *

Although Ripper's actions and the web of unconscious motives that produce them are important, they are, nevertheless, only one component of a larger system in which terror and rejection of the female devolve into the organization of a latent homosexual brotherhood whose behavior, even when it appears to be competitive, is a unified assault on femininity. Kubrick seems to be suggesting that the phallic–narcissistic ideal is actually an aberration that develops in response to an impairment in male potency and a consequent transformation of sexuality into sadism.

Here, the principal case in point is Dr. Strangelove, himself. As I noted earlier, the very name means perversion, and the character's impairment is not merely that he is a paraplegic, but that he is made of at least as much mechanical prosthesis as flesh and blood. If that were not enough, however, his mechanical nature is frequently in a life-or-death struggle with whatever human nature has survived in him. His literal emergence into the spotlight is brilliantly conceived. Our first sight of him is almost as an epiphany. He materializes from the shadows in response to a question from the president, the steel of his machinery gleaming against the chiaroscuro of the recess where he has been waiting, his teeth showing white in the frozen rictus of a grin, the lights glinting spookily off the his tinted glasses.

Lacking the capability for direct erotic experience, Strangelove has become a repository of inhibited desire fused with aggression, all under the domination of a brilliant, soulless, intellect and placed at the service of an internalized tyrannical and sadistic image that emerges with the title "Mein Führer." He refers to people as "human specimens," assures the president that the decision about who will be destroyed by the nuclear holocaust and who will be saved by descending into the mine shafts will be made, not by a sadistic Dr. Mengele, but by a computer, a machine, according to strict eugenic principles, and further, that the survivors would not be grief stricken because, "When they go down into the mine, everyone would still be alive. There would be no shocking memories, and the prevailing emotion would be one of nostalgia for those left behind, combined with a spirit of bold curiosity for the adventure ahead."

At this point, his right arm flexes into a Nazi salute and he pulls it back into his lap and beats at it. Suddenly, his dissociated gloved hand attempts to strangle him. There is a struggle within Strangelove between the machine and the man, between a dissociated, mechanistic ideology, and a human volition. It is as though he thrives on destructive energy, almost as though he materializes only when the world is at risk of annihilation, and he grows progressively stronger as the end approaches, like the character of Fedallah, the Parsee, in *Moby Dick* (Hayford & Parker, 1967, p. 187), hidden below decks by Ahab until the white whale is actually in sight. Strangelove thrives on destructiveness. His vitality is so enhanced by it that, in the end, this damaged, flaccid man becomes erect, as do all of the damaged phalluses of the film, under the stimulus of death.

*   *   *

The B-52 bomber is, itself, such a symbol. It is at once a phallus and a sperm cell, one of the many making their way towards Mother Russia. Like a sperm cell, it competes with myriad others that fail to reach the egg. Such is its persistence, however, that despite every conceivable deterrent, it succeeds. This is a grotesque parody of the process of conception where, instead of carrying the key to a new life, the plane is a messenger of total destruction. As such, it epitomizes the idea conveyed in a less comprehensive way by most of the male characters, that an inherent feature of men, and male-dominated institutions, is the exclusion of women and of feminine qualities from the sphere of their activity; when they succeed in doing this, their sexuality becomes fused with aggression. The result is that the same drive that might impel a sperm cell to overcome any and all obstacles to penetrate the ovum provides the indomitable urge to destruction. I think Kubrick is here urging the inevitability of annihilation when desire is derailed and fuses with aggression, and when the product of that fusion is both projected into an enemy and dissociated into technology.

Thus, the ultimate cause of the World's end is the so-called Doomsday Machine, a nuclear time bomb that cannot be disarmed. It is a relative of the computer that Dr. Strangelove would use to make all life and death decisions. It is also related to that moment in history when William the Conquerer thought it wise to accumulate vital information about all the inhabitants of his newly subjugated realm, and record it in what was called the Domesday Book (Williams & Martin, 2002), the earliest example of a national census for the purpose of controlling people.

That technology has the effect of denaturing life is a theme introduced when Ripper orders Mandrake to transmit plan R—for Robert—to the Wing. Robert is close enough to Robot to prefigure the situation that results from activating mechanical devices that follow their own sequences, each stage escalating inexorably to the next. As Strangelove gleefully describes it when commenting on the doomsday machine, "And so, because of the automated and irrevocable decision-making process which rules out human meddling, the doomsday machine is terrifying." The interpolation of layers of technology between the performance of a violent act and its effects is a system that renders mass destruction possible by a process of dissociation and disavowal. The robot becomes the engine of projected human viciousness.

* * *

This repudiation of responsibility for one's own aggression is woven into the fabric of the United States' masculine ideal. It is, thus, a stroke of genius for Kubrick to have chosen a cowboy to actually deliver the bomb. For who but a cowboy would embody the indigenously American version of machismo? And where but in Western films did generations of American men find their role models? The essence of the role model is that the good guy never starts a fight, but when provoked, he is an effective counter puncher and, in the extreme version often portrayed by Clint Eastwood, the avenging angel. This paradigm finds representation in the G. I. and the doughboy, no less than in the cowboy, but it is most cogently the archetype of the nation as a whole: the United States does not start wars, but we do finish them. We are the innocent naïves, the noble savage in such avatars as Natty Bumpo, George Washington, Huckleberry Finn, Billy Budd, Nick Adams, Abe Lincoln, Babe Ruth, Buffalo Bill, Jay Gatsby, Indiana Jones, John Wayne, Joe DiMaggio, Sargeant York, and Luke Skywalker—strong, fundamentally good men, provoked into becoming heroic by forces beyond themselves. We are untainted by the corruption of the Old World and, therefore, peculiarly vulnerable to its devious strategies, just as to the inherent treacheries of the Red Indian, and the Yellow Peril from the inscrutable Orient. We deal with internecine conflict by splitting and projection, like a good borderline personality who thus establishes the purity of his own motives while creating a license to be violent.

The film challenges this American icon by demonstrating that its sentimentality and romanticism are mere camouflage for far more sinister inclinations. It also deprives us of the Hollywood *deus-ex-machina* that always results in a happy ending, substituting for it the figure of Dr. Strangelove, a kind of *machina-ex-anthropos*, whose abrupt appearance implements a distinctly unhappy ending. Kubrick then adds insult to injury by remaining unremittingly comic: not only does he destroy the world but, while doing so, he denies us the refuge of high seriousness.

Major Kong, like his simian namesake, is an innocent. The sum of his acquired culture is that he's "been to one World's Fair, a picnic, and a rodeo." The speech he makes to his crew even acknowledges their humanity: "I got a fair idea of the kind of personal emotions some of you fellas may be thinkin. Heck, I reckon you wouldn't even be human beins' if you didn't have some pretty strong feelings about nuclear combat." However, the absurdity of his understatement emphasizes his basic inability to recognize the enormity of the situation, a quality that he shares in abundance with Turgidson and Bat Guano.

Kubrick makes sure we do not miss the point by having Kong next show his thirst for glory in reminding his men that they will be, "in line for some important promotions and personal citations when this thing is over." Finally, he delivers a parody on the stereotypic U.S. position on ethnic differences: "That goes for every last one of ya, regardless of race, color, or creed." Another tenet of the quintessential American hero is that, when the time comes to oppose the outside enemy, we are at our most tolerant and democratic. Kong's obliviousness to the implications of his behavior is nowhere more evident than when he rides the bomb down; with a phallus of such magnitude between his legs, how can he be anything but invincible? The point is that Kong is not a bad man or even a stupid man. He is just a cowboy doing his job. Was it not Hannah Arendt (1978) who coined the phrase "the banality of evil" to describe Adolf Eichmann?

A different kind of naïf is the character of Bat Guano whose central preoccupations are sexual deviation, chain of command, and private property. The very incarnation of what Joyce McDougall has termed "... he who is *afflicted with normality*" (1980, p. 468, original italics), he shows an unreasoning terror of the deviation that he sees everywhere and, like all the other characters, he stands in awe of the machine—in this case, a Coca Cola dispenser. He warns Mandrake that he cannot violate the machine's integrity by firing at it because it is private property and, should Mandrake fail to get the president on the phone, he will be answerable to the Coca Cola Company.

Here, at last, we discern the brutal values that lie beneath our heroic sentimentality. Homophobia and the intolerance of other para-sexualities are necessary to a society regimented against an outside enemy. As we have seen in the case of General Ripper, sexual deviation cannot be allowed because it is unconsciously equated with femininity, dependency, weakness, and helplessness. And the attribution of sacred qualities to private property as opposed to human life is the foundation of the willingness to immolate all, or a significant portion, of the world's population on the altar of that ultimate symbol of private property, the mega-corporation. Likewise, Turgidson objects to the Russian ambassador's being invited to the War Room on the grounds that, "He'll see the big board," the name we give to the most comprehensive emblem of private property, Wall Street's display of securities. Note, here, the parallel between the Big Board of Securities, which represents the things we must protect, and the Big Board of national security, which represents the boundaries we must defend in order to protect these things.

*   *   *

At this point, I should like to examine the character of the president, Merkin Muffley, and the problems he presents for the interpretation of the film. In contrast to the ostentatious machismo of Turgidson, Ripper, Guano, Kong, and even Strangelove himself, stands the apparently reasonable, humane, to some degree ineffectual, figure of Muffley. Some commentators on the film have likened him to Adlai Stevenson, who unsuccessfully opposed President Eisenhower in 1952 and 1956, and later served as the U.S. ambassador to the United Nations. It can be argued that Kubrick is illustrating Yeats' aphorism that "the best lack all conviction while the worst are full of passionate intensity" (1983a, pp. 187–188). But, in calling him Merkin Muffley (literally, the female pubic area with a false hair piece), Kubrick seems to be adopting the macho perspective himself. That is, he labels the president as a female, using epithets that betray the same fear and contempt for femininity as the characters whom he intends as the targets of his satire. Where the tough guys all have luxuriant heads of hair, Muffley is bald; the configuration of lights above the huge round table in the War Room echoes the fringe of hair surrounding Merkin's bare skull, and also the shapes of the mushroom clouds whose graceful, choreographed eruptions form the film's final tableau.

*   *   *

The original target of the B-52 bomber was Laputa, a locale borrowed from Jonathan Swift's *Gulliver's Travels* (1940, pp. 141–205), in which it is a mythical country—a flying island whose inhabitants were given to visionary, fanciful, and absurd projects. In Spanish, the word *laputa* means "whore." Again, the attack is against the female. Are these elements of the film (the president's name, personality, baldness; vaginal symbols in the design of the War Room, the nuclear explosions, the name of the target, and the almost complete absence of women characters) simply random inconsistencies that somehow eluded the eye of Stanley Kubrick, who was known for his obsessive attention to, and control of, every detail of his work? Or, can they be read as intrusions from his own unconscious fear and hatred of women? Although it would be difficult to find the definitive answer to the question I have just posed, we can consider it in the light of my discussion of the rest of the film. I have suggested that the work attempts to show how some of the central values of our society—machismo, the proliferation of technology, strategies of social control, intolerance of deviance, the disavowal of aggression, a patriarchal structure, gynephobia, unacknowledged paraphelic impulses, the fetishization of private property, xenophobia, and rugged individualism—could, taken to an extreme, result in world destruction. Might it be that Kubrick was able to elucidate the problem but, because of his own unconscious identification with the very values he was skewering, he could not but join the attack on the female principle?

*   *   *

Mention should be made of the use of music in the film. During the opening credits, against the background of the mid-air copulation, we hear an orchestral arrangement of the pop song, "Try a Little Tenderness" (Redding, 1998). Now, although this seems funny, it is, on reflection, simply another sidelong snicker at women. Each time we see the bomber, the accompaniment is the tune we have learned to identify as "When Johnny Comes Marching Home" (Leonard, 2007). But this is an Americanized version of an older Irish song in which the words were not, "We'll give him a hearty welcome then, hurrah, hurrah . . . and we'll all feel gay when Johnny comes marching home;" but, rather, "Where are your eyes that were so mild, haroo, haroo . . . with their guns and drums and drums and guns / the enemy nearly slew ye / Oh my darling dear, ye look so queer / Johnny, I hardly knew ye" (www.ireland-information.com). The music in the final sequence is a swing arrangement of the popular Second World War tune, "We'll Meet Again Some Sunny Day" (Parker & Charles, 1939). The lyrics are, "We'll meet again, / don't know where, / don't know when, / but I know we'll meet again some sunny day."

Ironically, there will never be a sunnier day than the one on which multiple nuclear explosions engender what one Hiroshima observer described as "the light of a thousand suns." Using actual footage of the original Trinity test in 1945, other atmospheric explosions, and the Bikini Atoll blast, Kubrick creates an image that is at once terrifying and serene, with the surreal beauty of the synchronized swimming of an Esther Williams film, a Busby Berkeley production number, or, longer ago, the fireworks and light shows of the Worlds' Fairs or the timing of the fountains at Versailles. That is, he provides a grand finale that is both the end of the film and the end of the world. But it is an aesthetic end, as if to say that in no art is man more proficient than the art of destruction. Kubrick contradicts Eliot: the world ends with a bang, not with a whimper. And there will be no next time.

Up in the Air: The unfriendly skies

The essence of *Up in the Air* is in the meanings of the critical events in Ryan Bingham's life. The opening credits are run against a backdrop of abstract landscape seen from high in the air. The features are intensely beautiful, consisting of geometric shapes and saturated colors, but they bear no relation to the life of the planet from the perspective of a participant. The implication is that, for Ryan Bingham, the film's protagonist, the harmonies visible from seven miles up are preferable to the chaos and conflict of life at sea level.

The seamlessness of Earth from above corresponds to Ryan's zip-up–button-down style in which no fractals mar the smooth contours of his luggage or image. This, of course, changes when the unwieldy cut-out of his sister and brother-in-law protrudes. The world that Ryan loves, we often hate, but we envy his mastery of it. It is a world of rigorous structure, stripped to essentials, regimented, ritualized, and alienated.

* * *

Ryan's personal derailment begins when the flight attendant asks him, "Do you want the can, sir?" eliding the last two syllables so that they sound like "cancer." Though he recovers quickly, Ryan is shaken by the implication that reality, in the form of serious illness, may penetrate even so inviolable a place as the first-class section of his airliner. The second sign of trouble is his assistant's inability to book him a full-sized car despite his being a highly privileged customer of the rental company. Next, he receives a disquieting communication from his boss that there are radical changes afoot in the way the business is conducted. The boss's complaint of constipation is another variation on the theme of physical infirmity and vulnerability to "the thousand natural shocks that flesh is heir to" (Shakespeare, 1958, p. 63). Finally, during one of his rare nights at home, the woman next door, who has clearly been available to him for casual sex, refuses him, explaining that she is seeing someone else.

Ryan's relationship with Alex begins as competition and narcissistic mirroring. They compare credit and privilege cards and the power and sexuality that these symbolize. But it is difficult to determine whether the cards really represent sexuality and power or have been sublimated to a condition of functional autonomy. It is in this scene that we begin to understand that Ryan's sense of values is predicated not on materialism but on an abstract principle, the attainment of ten million miles as an end in itself, as well as on the concept of loyalty. After the card comparison, the actual matching and evaluation of genitals, no matter how exciting, had to have been anticlimactic (as it were) to these connoisseurs of credit and privilege. The mirroring is accentuated in the profile shot of their dueling laptops as well as Alex's later remark, "Think of me as yourself, only with a vagina."

After their first meeting, Ryan, the presumed master of one-night stands, says, "We gotta do this again." The intimations of fleshly weakness and illness foreshadow this dawning evidence of what he would construe as an emotional weakness, the susceptibility to attachment that is so alien to what we have learned of Ryan's personality. Two sets of circumstances converge to penetrate Ryan's armor against relatedness. The first is his developing feeling for Alex; the second is his taking on the task of educating Natalie to the realities of the work they do and, in the process, exposing her humanity and having to minister to it. When her boyfriend severs their relationship in a text message, we recognize the parallel to her own scheme for firing people on the internet. With Ryan as her mentor, Natalie learns from these experiences and is changed by them. Ryan asks Natalie, "What is it you think we do here?" Natalie answers, "We prepare the newly unemployed for the emotional and physical hurdles of job hunting while minimizing legal blowbacks." Ryan corrects her: "That's what we're selling; it's not what we're doing." Natalie asks, " Okay, what are we doing?" Ryan says, "We are here to make limbo tolerable, to ferry wounded souls across the river of dread to the point where hope is dimly visible and then stop the boat, shove 'em in the water and make 'em swim." Later, he adds, "This is what we do, Natalie, we take people at their most fragile and we set them adrift."

*   *   *

The implication is that Ryan is also changed. His forced engagement with Natalie's feelings paves the way for progressively deeper, more affective involvement with Alex, with his own family, and, ultimately, with himself.

The experience he has and what he learns from it are the crux of the movie. The plot's arc begins with Ryan as a confirmed loner and antagonist of commitment. It develops and rises when, by degrees, he becomes ever more deeply involved with people and the feelings that link him to them. The climax occurs when he is painfully rejected. And the denouement consists of his acceptance of his place in the clouds, but changed by what he has been through. He has loved and lost, but he *has* loved and this has changed his attitude and his understanding of his place in the world.

Ryan never returns to his previously comfortable level of activity. When the chief pilot asks him where he is from, there is a wistful hesitation before he replies, "I'm from here," that is, from the sky and the cabin and the airline culture. The implication is that he has severed his last fragile link to the ground.

The Ryan we meet early in the film is trapped in the myriad routines and rituals of his mission. Thought is alien to him. He functions as an automaton. Just as his patented interventions abruptly derail the lives of those he fires, so do circumstances conspire to derail his own life. It is at this point that he begins to feel and think, and change.

The precipitating events occur in the essential domains of love and work. His static personal equilibrium is upset by his deepening feelings for Alex and his static professional equilibrium is threatened by Natalie's proposed changes in the company's *modus operandi*. Both are further potentiated by his reluctant engagement with his family and recruitment for the incongruous role of persuading his future brother-in-law to honor his commitment, a task diametrically opposite his accustomed one of counseling distance and separateness.

As we see, Ryan's wish to abolish the boundary between the road relationship with Alex and a more comprehensive one involving a life together founders on her unavailability. He handles the threat to his profession by using his initiative, knowledge, and skill to demonstrate how the new method, the interpolation of an additional layer of technology between the firer and the fired, is flawed. He learns from both sets of experiences. He returns to the heavens chastened by the knowledge that his is not the best of all possible lives, that he has left a better one behind, that he has lost something of inestimable value. His attitude to people has been radically changed, too. Despite the necessary function he performs of severing them from their vocational roots, he feels compassion and empathy for them because he has now been one of them.

*   *   *

The character, Ryan Bingham, is not a man; he is the angel of death, or the commercial equivalent. It is his job to tell people they are finished. By doing so, he disillusions them at a single stroke about their security, the continuity of their existence, and their entitlement to a stake in the American dream. He reminds them that everything comes to an end and thereby forces them to acknowledge the reality of death.

One of the problems with American culture is that it makes no provision for engaging death. Instead, it treats the subject with phobic avoidance. This phenomenon is epitomized in Scott Fitzgerald's prophetic novel, *The Great Gatsby* (2003, p. 180), from the last page of which I quote:

> And as I sat there brooding on the old, unknown world, I thought of Gatsby's wonder when he first picked out the green light at the end of Daisy's dock. He had come a long way to this blue lawn and his dream must have seemed so close that he could hardly fail to grasp it. He did not know that it was already behind him, somewhere back in that vast obscurity beyond the city where the dark fields of the republic rolled on under the night. Gatsby believed in the green light, the orgiastic future that year by year recedes before us. It eluded us then, but that's no matter—tomorrow we will run faster, stretch out our arms farther . . . And one fine morning—So we beat on, boats against the current, borne back ceaselessly into the past.

Gatsby's belief, and that of his fellow Americans, is echoed and reinforced by the dictum of Vince Lombardi (n.d.), the legendary football coach, who said, "I never lost a football game; it's just that time ran out." That is, instead of accepting loss, failure, and disappointment, and learning from them, Americans tend never to say die. This is both a strength and a weakness: strength in that it constitutes an admirable persistence even against formidable obstacles, weakness in being an impediment to thought and self-reflection.

In opposition to the perspective expressed in the quotation from *Gatsby*, we have two other archetypal works of literature—one Hindu, the other Christian—that focus on the crucial moment at which a person's quotidian experience is suddenly fractured by an anomalous event. The Hindu poem *Bhagavad Gita* (Mitchell, 2000), describes how a great prince is abruptly forced to reflect on his life moments before he is to lead his army into battle. *Hell*, or *Inferno*, the first book of *La Commedia*, by Dante, is the account of a man who, in midlife, becomes lost in a dark wood, unable to find his way. He chooses to enter a gate, above which is the inscription "Abandon hope, ye who enter here" (Alighieri, 1951, p. 17). He is motivated by the combination of despair and curiosity.

Ryan Bingham says to one of the men whom he must fire, "I'm not a shrink, I'm a wakeup call." In this sense, he resembles Jacques Lacan, who would occasionally terminate his patients' sessions after a few minutes to remind them that things come to an end and that psycho-analysis, like life, is not interminable. As the angel of death, Ryan offers people a *memento mori*, literally, "Remember, you shall die!" He gives no quarter and asks for none. There is no appeal from the news he brings.

Ryan is not a shrink because he does all of his work in a single session. If he succeeds, his client will change her life; if he does not succeed, his client may simply find another job, or take her own life, as one of them actually does. His admonition to them is, "Anyone who ever built an empire or changed the world sat where you are now and it's because they sat there that they were able to do it, and that's the truth."

It is, indeed, the truth and also the principle that emerges from the great literary treatments of the consequences of personal crisis: if you do not wake up from your illusions and confront the nature of your existence, you will sleep in ignorance forever. If you do not live, you will never be able to accept death: "the horror of death is the horror of dying with what Rilke called unlived lines in our bodies" (Brown, 1959, p. 197).

In fact, much of the advice that Ryan gives has value if the recipient is able to hear it. He urges people to travel light by burning all the baggage they carry through life. "Begin with the photos," he says, "Photos are for people who can't remember." Is he referring here to object constancy and to the tourists of life who are so busy taking pictures of it that they do not experience it?

Ryan inherits the tradition of the Lone Ranger, John Wayne, James Bond, and the spaghetti Western version of Clint Eastwood. The crucial difference between Ryan and these larger-than-life heroes is that in him, and in this film, we get to study the psychology of the archetype rather than simply watching it at work. We also discover that, unlike these counterparts, Ryan wants commitment but is rejec-ted. The other heroes, in contrast, prefer a male sidekick, one-night stands, or they lose the woman who matters when she is killed. Not uncommonly, this species of hero leaves the woman who loves him in a paroxysm of self-sacrifice. The prototype for this way of repudiating intimacy is Sidney Carton in Dickens's (1996, p. 454), *A Tale of Two Cities*, who says, "It is a far, far better thing that I do, than I have ever done; it is a far, far better rest that I go to than I have ever known" before sacrificing himself for the woman he loves by replacing the man she loves under the guillotine. His double in Western films is Shane.

The work that Ryan does, forcing a caesura, calling an end to something, is very difficult. If it were not, the bosses and HR departments who hire him would do it themselves. This reluctance to wield the axe or scalpel may be regarded as a metaphor for a more general and abstemious avoidance of being seen or experienced as the agent of termination or rejection. Witness the way in which the termination of a treatment remains an unsolved enigma even after a century of work by the profession's best minds. To put an end to anything is tantamount to killing, administering a *coup de grâce*. As a result, unless the end is preconceived or institutional, as the end of a work day, a semester at school, a game or a chartered period of time, such as a day or year, it can only be attained with great conflict and pain. In the latter category we may put divorce, the rupture of all relationships, going to sleep, moving, and, most relevant for this discussion, termination of employment.

What we are witness to in *Up in the Air* is the transformations wrought in the character of a paid assassin, a hit man of business, the angel of death, from being a heartless machine to a compassionate being. What we do not witness is a change in his profession, because what he does is necessary and extremely difficult, especially now that he can no longer anesthetize himself either to his own pain or that of his victims.

It would be consistent with Hollywood's compulsion to preempt meaning by means of sentimentality, if Ryan had either given up his profession or remained unaffected by his derailment experiences. It is the strength of this film that, though he has been made able to feel, he must nevertheless continue to perform the function of cutting people off from one of their critical supports, an act that epitomizes mortality and the essential tragedy of human existence. The gunslinger continues to kill innocents because even the innocent must die. He is not reformed, punished, or eliminated. But he is enlightened. We, too, are enlightened. We learn that death is real and that the dread we feel at every lesser ending is nothing more than a reminder of it.

Another message we can take from *Up in the Air* is that there are alternate modes of being and relating and that certain transformations are prerequisites to effective intimacy. Perhaps what we are dealing with here is the universal conflict between excitement and security, both quintessential human needs. Alex says to Natalie, after her boyfriend has jilted her, "Pricks are spontaneous, they're unpredictable, and they're fun. Then we're surprised when they turn out to be pricks." She is underscoring that there are times when the other's capacity to excite is more important than security. Let's recall, in this context, Robert Stoller's (1975) conclusion that, without a measure of hatred and perversion, sex becomes boring. Alex says to Ryan, "Back home, I don't get to act the way I do with you," to which Ryan responds, "That's why I don't have a back home."

Here, however, is the rub. Alex does have a back home. She has both the excitement and the security. In this sense, the role she assumes is more akin to that of a man conducting an extra-marital affair. Ryan evolves to the point where he wants to have a back home with Alex. He says to her, "I don't know what originally sparked the backpack. Probably needed to be alone. Recently, I've been thinking that I needed to empty the backpack before I knew what to put back in it." The significance of this exchange is that it is exceedingly difficult, if not impossible to have a truly intimate experience unless one has first been able to be alone, to individuate. In my work with couples, much of the dyadic discord is caused by the incompleteness of individuation in one or both partners, and the impediment that presents as a wish for a different type of partner is often a disguised longing for absent or failed experiences of individuation.

In view of these considerations, I propose that there are developmental issues that are crucial to our understanding of intimacy and its vicissitudes. First, it is not a question of narcissism or individualism in any generic sense but, rather, that a certain species of narcissism is the outcome of failure in the process of individuation. That young people, generally, and young men, in particular, may be mistakenly taken to be excessively narcissistic and individualistic is often a function of their being observed *in vivo* as they struggle to attain a personal identity. Because a modicum of security is necessary for the conduct of this struggle, many young adults marry or partner with someone to whom they unconsciously assign the role of the idealized parent who will successfully catalyze their individuation where the real parent did not, for whatever reason.

This is a central theme that the film offers for our consideration.

Tunes of Glory: To march and to mourn

Ronald Neames' film, *Tunes of Glory*, made in 1960 and based on a novel by James Kennaway (1956) is, at first glance, a study of the splits between male and female, educated and working classes, war and peace, and charismatic *vs.* bureaucratic leadership. The male–female split is introduced in the opening credits when Morag Sinclair, the acting Colonel's daughter, enters the forbidden all-male perimeter of the barracks, in violation of the boundaries set by the institution of the military, and, more explicitly and personally, by her own father. She is there because of her attachment to the young piper, Corporal Fraser, and she is cautioned against this liaison by the Pipe Major, Mr. McClain, an oracular figure whose warnings go unheeded. The film, then, begins with a violation of the taboo against a female presence in the male garrison.

Immediately following this, Jock hazes the young lieutenant for smoking a cigarette like a debutante instead of inhaling it, "Like a man," underscoring the premium on masculinity among the soldiers. This provides a neat segue into the theme of class opposition, as Jock, addressing two educated officers, asks, "Am I coarse, Simpson? Am I, Charlie?" And while ridiculing Charlie's "Old boy" by sarcastic imitation, Jock makes it very clear that the only title to be used in the officers' mess is his own, "Colonel." His is an old boys' network that would be more approved among southern rednecks than graduates of Eton.

We soon learn that Jock's appointment as acting Colonel was the result of his spontaneous battlefield heroism in the Second World War, as opposed to Barrow's appointment as Colonel, which came, presumably, through the channels of army bureaucracy. Thus, the theme of two opposing leadership perspectives, charismatic *vs.* bureaucratic, is introduced.

Although the relation between war and peace is subtly broached earlier in the film, it receives its clearest introduction in Barrow's speech to the officers in which he states, "Before the war, the social responsibilities of an officer greatly outweighed his military duties; the last thing I want to do is to reestablish that order. We are, first and foremost, soldiers." He then adds, however, that, though they are tough men in war, they must be gentlemen in peace, and goes on to implement this principle with prescriptions for gentlemanly dancing.

The film's central conflict is set forth dramatically in the announcement Sinclair makes to his officers at what is, in effect, his farewell party. He declares that the battalion is to have a new Colonel who will replace him as its commander. Assuming that the Colonel will arrive the next day, the officers continue their revels. They dance to the skirling pipes, some assuming the role of females, so designated by a handkerchief tied around their forearms. One of these is Dusty, the mess president, whose sexual ambiguity is established by his wearing the kerchief, but also trousers rather than a kilt, and, later, during the early morning dance practice, by the descent of his pajama pants from their unseen position above the hem of his kilt, to their full ankle length, by the motion of his body. His partner at Jock's party takes the role of a man, though he wears a kilt, and Dusty, that of a woman, though he is wearing pants. One of the problems for these tough fighting men is how to establish and maintain the boundaries that allow them to keep their own femininity at bay.

They do so in many ways. First, women have no place in their barracks. (Jock tells his daughter, Morag, "There's only one kind of girl hangs around a barracks.") Clearly, that kind of girl does not violate the male–female boundary but, on the contrary, reinforces it. Second, when respectable women *are* allowed into the barracks, as at Barrow's cocktail party, they are treated sadistically and aggressively. Third, there is to be no soft or feminine behavior among the troops: the Lieutenant is not allowed to smoke like a debutante. He must inhale like a man. The entire battalion drinks whiskey. When Barrow tells Jock that he does not, he is seen as unmanly. Jock uses the word "wee" as a damning epithet. It refers to a man's size and, by implication, that of his equipment. There are to be no concessions to external authority: the battalion settles its own conflicts "like men." "If you have honorable intentions towards your lassie, you're a bloody fool," barks Jock at Corporal Fraser. Honorable intentions constitute a dangerous bridge to the feminine. Gentlemen and gentlemanly behavior must be ridiculed and discouraged: it is a reminder of the feminine. Thus, "Old boy; toy soldier; Oxford graduate; taught at Sandhurst; whatever it is that gentlemen shoot at when they go shooting, etc., etc."

The contrast between Jock and Barrow is nowhere more telling than in their respective wartime activities. Jock's leadership of the battalion was established in the North African Desert, where he acted with aggressive heroics, catapulted into his role by the vicissitudes of battle. The implication is that he was not the acting Colonel until the circumstances of the war against Rommel recruited his particular rough and ready personality into its particular niche. In less critical times, he might have risen no higher than the Pipe Major. Barrow, on the other hand, was a prisoner of war, rendered helpless and tortured nearly to death by his captors, having to endure terror, pain, and humiliation with a passive, stoical resistance. His confession to Jimmy after their ride in the jeep suggests that although he survived physically, he died spiritually. Translated into psychoanalytic symbols, this implies castration. Accordingly, Barrow is a castrated, bureaucratic, gentlemanly, feminized figure alongside Jocks phallic–narcissistic, charismatic, working class, ostentatiously masculine image.

Having observed these opposites, we are nevertheless forced by the material of the film to notice that there are intimations that they are less than absolute. For example, when Jock is troubled, he turns to a woman, Mary, for solace, albeit he has been at considerable pains to avoid her for a significant period. Were he not suffering, he would not seek her out. We discover that she has never been allowed to come to his house or to meet his daughter and we recall that when his daughter alluded to Mary, he exploded in anger. On his first visit to Mary, he does not reveal his need but does mention the humiliation of Barrow's dance-practice sessions. He is quickly rejected by an offended Mary and ridiculed with a parody of battalion dancing. His second visit to Mary is more urgent: he is frightened because he has committed the severely punishable offense of striking a non-commissioned officer in uniform, in public. He needs her support and comfort, but finding her entertaining Charlie Scott, he leaves with the air of one who is poorly concealing hurt feelings. In the third encounter with Mary, it is she who breaks the taboo by coming to his house unbidden and giving him the strength to fight for his military position rather than capitulate to a court martial. She indicates that he is the best man she has ever known, a brave man, and reminds him of his own resilience. She needs to idealize him and he needs her nurturance. Even so, there is a moment when his reflexive allegiance to the masculine principle results in a mistrustful repudiation of Mary, but he quickly apologizes.

Likewise, there are other contradictory bits of dialogue throughout the film that caution us to avoid a too facile view of the male–female antimony. Alone with Charlie in the wee hours after his party, Jock says, "You nurse them from Alamein to Casino, from Berlin to Dover just to get some wee spry gent put over your head at the end." When Jock returns to the mess after learning that he is to be disciplined at the brigade level for his transgression in striking Corporal Fraser, he asks who will have lunch with him. The first three officers who agree to accompany him are warmly embraced and referred to as, "my babies," a peculiarly maternal epithet from so macho a man. And, if this were not enough, in the final dramatic scene at which Barrow's funeral is being planned, Jock, dissolved in helpless weeping, exclaims, "All my babies."

It appears that Jock unconsciously perceives himself as the mother of the battalion. He was elevated to this position by the circumstances of war, which demanded a leader whose raw courage and resilience could rescue his men from destruction, a figure who could "nurse them from Alamein to Casino . . ." in the sense of nurture them and minister to their hurts. He accomplished this with the toughness and the single-minded aggression that he displays during the entire action of the film. The bond between him and the men of the battalion was forged in the white heat of battle. That Jock, though a parent, never mentions his wife, contrasts with Barrow's indicating to Jimmy that he was once married. Jock is both father and mother; Barrow's marriage was apparently barren.

In his insistence on isolating Morag from the barracks, Jock implements the split between his machismo and his consciously repudiated vulnerability, which he identifies with femininity. He projects this part of himself into his daughter and forbids her to have contact with the tough, soldierly part of his world. Accordingly, his violent response to seeing Morag and Corporal Fraser together at the bar represents the climax of the film, the point at which many of the well-guarded boundaries are weakened and breached: the event foreshadowed in the film's opening scene when Morag visits the garrison. From here to the end of the film, the consequences of this loss of boundaries are explored until we discover its cause and ultimate meaning.

A crucial variation on the theme of boundaries is introduced when Barrow violates the time set for his arrival and intrudes on Jock's party. His subsequent attempts to cross the boundary by assuming titular command and influencing the officers' behavior are met with serial failure and he is painfully excluded from their *esprit-de-corps*.

This trajectory, as we know, ends in his suicide, following a devastating conversation with Charlie in the billiard room.

Barrow's goal is not merely to become colonel to the battalion, but to affect its transition from an instrument of war to a guardian in peace. To do this, he must wrest power from the war leader and transform the ethos of the men from belligerence to civility. That he is not up to the task is obvious, but the sequelae of his failure remain to be explained.

Jock's problem is that the very qualities that equipped him for leadership in war are antagonistic to the postwar functions of the unit. His tragic flaw is that, unable to adapt to the change, he must, therefore, play out his indigenous role like some anachronistic juggernaut. He takes the battalion with him in doing so. But they follow him because he has led them through many dangerous situations and because they, too, are so hyper-adapted for war that they cannot demobilize themselves. This problem is graphically represented in their dancing: theirs is a war dance, and when asked to transform it to the social usages of peacetime, they cannot.

So, the contrast between Barrow and Sinclair is multifaceted. Barrow is obsessional and anal retentive, Jock is anal expulsive and phallic–narcissistic. Barrow is bureaucratic and aloof; Jock is charismatic and egalitarian. Barrow operates by the book; Jock, by the seat of his pants. The discussion between Mr. McClain, the Pipe Major, and Mr. Riddick, the Warrant Officer, is telling. Riddick, himself anal retentive (witness his accusing the little soldier carrying the tea kettle of being "dirty"), favors Barrow because he is a "gentleman;" McClain calls Riddick a snob and suggests that this attitude was typical in his former regiment. Riddick bridles and offers to fight McClain who counters with a scornful remark. But the point is made that officers are expected to act like, if not actually be, gentlemen. In this regard, recall McClain's admonishing Jock for having done a stupid thing by hitting Corporal Fraser.

It is interesting to consider Charlie Scott's position relative to Jock and Barrow. Clearly, he has never approved of Jock. We become aware of this from his response to Jock's "Am I coarse?" following the hazing of the young lieutenant in the opening scene. Charlie does not answer and, throughout the film, he maintains an aristocratic aloofness from Jock even while remaining his friend and confidant. That Jock is fully aware of this attitude is reflected in his constant sarcastic echoing of

Charlie's "Old boy," and by his half-jocular reproach that Charlie does not talk and is not even a good listener. When Barrow elicits his opinion regarding the appropriate response to Jock's offense in striking the Corporal, he advises strict disciplinary action through official channels. In urging this, he is nowise deterred by ties of friendship or loyalty to Jock. The quintessence of Charlie's personality is his coolness. In the billiard room, after his devastating conversation with Barrow, and with Jock pressuring him, he takes unflinching aim and makes a perfect shot, demonstrating extraordinary grace under fire. Why, then, has Charlie, the second in command, a gentleman, and an excellent officer, not been given the opportunity for promotion to Colonel? The logic of the situation would prohibit this because he would have to go up against Jock; but there is perhaps a more compelling reason. His very coolness, his *sang froid*, the quality that would make him technically qualified, would not inspire the kind of loyalty and trust that Jock, in his more emotionally accessible style, can command. In part, Charlie's role awaits the outcome of the conflict between Barrow and Jock. He certainly understands this and his actions are geared to the possibility of taking command when the other two have defeated each other and themselves.

Before this can happen, however, the battalion must experience another event that will catalyze a critical transformation in its emotional life. The suicide of Colonel Barrow marks the onset of this process. After the gunshot is heard, Jock sends the young officer to investigate. He reports his findings and Jock goes upstairs with him. There, in the shower room, they enact a remarkable scene over the corpse of Colonel Barrow. Jock asks the young man, "Laddie, are you going to faint?" "Aye," says the boy.

"Well, don't be ashamed," succors Jock. After a moment, the boy says, "I don't think so, sir," to which Jock replies, "Then you can make your debut." He adds, "If you're going to be a soldier, you must learn to handle both the living and the dead."

The scene is the counterpart of the very early one where Jock chides this same officer for smoking like a debutante, and not like a man. Here, under fire, we see a different Jock than the bluff bully of the officers' mess, someone who can accompany the young man in the rite of passage, who does so with kindness as well as toughness.

But it is the next line, "If you're going to be a soldier, you must learn to handle both the living and the dead," that provides the crucial *entrée* into the task that has so far eluded the battalion—that of mourning. Until now, under the stringent demands of action, the men have had all they can do to fight and survive the war. They have had neither the opportunity nor the structural changes that are necessary for the work of mourning. And this is why, when Jock says, "It is not the body that worries me; it's the ghost," he is not referring merely to a sense of guilt over Barrow's death, but to his own awareness that all the unmourned dead of the battalion are haunting it with their ghosts. In this sense, his advice to the young officer is cautionary for himself and the battalion: a soldier must deal with both the living and dead. Part of what was learned most dramatically after Vietnam and less dramatically after other wars, was that soldiers who cannot mourn cannot return to civilian life, cannot be restored to a fully human status. And this has been the battalion's dilemma: mobilized for war, with a warrior leader, how does it adapt to peace? A supreme irony is that Barrow, the living dead man, and the dead dead man, attains his lifelong wish after suicide—for a brief moment, he assumes leadership of the battalion, marching it under the lintel of mourning.

Earlier, in his private conversation with Jock, Barrow emphasizes, "It's the idea of the battalion: the living and the dead." In all organizations, but especially in the military, where sudden, violent death is frequent, and where the need for precipitous action precludes mourning, the dead are a constant presence. Recall, too, Jock's referring to himself as a ghost. "You see before you, Corporal, the body of a major and the ghost of a colonel." Manifestly, he has lost his rank with the advent of Barrow, but latently he is referring to the deadening of himself and others that is caused by war. Thus, it is not only the dead, but the survivors, too, who take on the status of ghosts.

The theme of mourning emerges with startling and deeply affecting clarity in the final scene of the film, where Jock has assembled the officers to plan Barrow's funeral. It is a very different Jock Sinclair who presides over this meeting, one who has incorporated Barrow's identification with the history and tradition of the battalion, "The idea of the battalion: the living and the dead," with its implicit imperative to metabolize the traumas of violence and death into products that foster further development. The inability to mourn, that is, cripples the personality by fixation on the defenses against the traumatic event. In the case of the battalion, these defenses consist of hard drinking, machismo, the exclusion of women, unquestioning loyalty, charismatic leadership, and a phallic–narcissistic ideal. The leader in war must succeed in suppressing all tendencies to grieve and mourn in order to mobilize and channel aggressive energies. In this context, witness the story of the sergeant in the First World War who, when his men hesitated to leave the safety of their trench and go "over the top," exhorted them by shouting, "Come on you sons of bitches, do you want to live forever?" (said to have been yelled by Sergeant Major Daniel Joseph "Dan" Daly, a United States Marine). Jock was a leader who was able to do this. In the final scene, he undoes it.

The other officers regard Jock's vision of Barrow's funeral as inappropriate. This is because they do not understand the underlying meaning that he intends the ritual to convey. He says, "We'll have all the tunes of glory to remember the more clearly. Sure we will," because the work of mourning has memory as its *metier* and it is only by remembering the dead and their deaths that their ghosts can be exorcised. He continues, "A whole battalion coming home." The image is a symbol of death, transformation, and reconciliation; it condenses the deaths of men who fell in war with the unmetabolized death in the personalities of the survivors, the notion of homecoming with its dual connotations of comfort and death with the need for integration between the experiences of destruction and the imperatives of reconstruction.

Finally, Jock rehearses the ritual to the off-camera sounds of the pipes and drums, and then to the drums alone as he paces rigidly towards the wall to the uttered cadence "Dit dit . . . die; dit dit . . . die," with its heartbreaking echo of the rhythms of wartime soldiering. His last words are a lament for the lost, the fallen, and the deadened under his command: "All my babies," he cries, and bursts into tears. Jimmy and the unflappable Charlie minister to their leader, now undone by the return of the repressed and its attendant suffering. As he has brought the battalion home, it is they who must now take him home.

Since the film is set in Scotland and peopled by Scots, there are the inevitable associations with Shakespeare's *Macbeth* (1989) in the central character's illegitimate aspiration to the rank of the highest leader, his fear of ghosts, and the hand-washing incident after he has made sure that Barrow is dead. Macbeth was also a war hero who was not content with his postwar status and who murdered to achieve his ends. The similarities are sufficient to provide the somewhat familiar frame of reference, the sense of fate and repetition that gives tragedy its peculiar resonance and transcendence, but not so much as to detract from the film's freshness and originality.

The Scottish milieu also makes possible the rich ambiguities of gender that are a visual representation of the dilemma of female exclusion from the garrison. Mel Brooks made a film titled *Robin Hood: Men in Tights* (1993); this film, if redone as comedy, might be called *Rob Roy: Men in Skirts.* Another title that would be apt is that of Hemingway's earliest book of stories, *Men Without Women* (1955), which, in itself, sheds further light on the dilemma of gender in this context. If you are going to write a book about soldiers and war, why include *Women* in your title? The answer, of course, is that you can never exclude women and that the female principle that is associated with experiences such as emotion, mourning, and being comforted, is nowhere more conspicuous than in its deliberate exclusion. If men are brutalized by war, their humanity must be restored by the healing affects of mourning administered by women.

The title, *Tunes of Glory*, is sufficiently close to "paths of glory" to evoke the line, "the paths of glory lead but to the grave" (Gray, 1964, p. 188). The importance of these "tunes" is emphasized throughout the film by the sounds of the pipes, and it must be noted that these are the same songs that both lead men into battle and serve, after the battle, as dirges. The skirl of the pipes is an accompaniment to war and a constant reminder of the coming home, the return to earth. General McArthur (1951) quoted a song to the effect that, "old soldiers never die," but *Tunes of Glory* reminds us that all soldiers die, some literally and some by the destruction of the capacity to feel.

CHAPTER THREE

Love and lust

The four films I have grouped under the heading "Love and lust", depict a spectrum that includes limerence, perversion, romance, stalking, affection, delusion, obsession, seduction, reverence, the myriad permutations of these and other variants of desire. They explore these states from the positions of their subjects and objects, but, more pointedly, in consideration of the projective and introjective processes that reverberate between them.

For example, the couple in *An Affair of Love* (Fonteyne, 1999a), initially strangers, meet for the purpose of enacting a perverse fantasy. They soon discover that their projections interfere with this endeavor. The results of projection and introjection are even more remarkable in *Certified Copy* (Kiarostami, 2010), which develops entirely according to the characters' unstable expectations of each other, with scarcely any attention to external conditions. Of the four films, *Talk to Her* (Almodóvar, 2002) departs most radically in representing the convolutions of desire by focusing on relations in which one of the two partners is comatose. This situation enables projection and introjection to become the sole relational vehicles.

Gods and Monsters (Condon, 1998) begins with clash of assumptions between the two principal characters: James Whale assumes that

Clayton Boone is a brute whose homophobia can be exploited into murder. Boone assumes that Whale is "an old fruit" who wants to seduce him. Neither can predict how their engagement will alter these assumptions

These films partake, inevitably, of the time-and-death theme, but to a subordinate degree, since all but two of the principals live on after their involvement with each other. Duration, however, is as integral to the structure of intimate relations as the affects and sensations of which they are composed; attachment and passion always include the possibility and often the certainty of loss, the shadow of which deepens all narratives. And every loss is a reminder of the final one.

An Affair of Love: Erotic variations

This film's plot turns on the acting out of a perverse fantasy which is contrasted with "normal sex," and the type of conventional love relationship in which it is deemed to occupy a central role and function. A woman places a personal ad in a sex magazine asking to meet with a man to engage in an unusual erotic activity, the nature of which remains unspecified to us, the audience.

Significantly, the film's original French title is *Une Liaison Pornographique* (Fonteyne, 1999b). The decision to alter it to *An Affair of Love* was certainly ill-advised because it introduces the film's principal complication prematurely, and gives it more weight than the story is meant to support. From the beginning, the process of fetishization and its impediments are made explicit. In his first meeting with the unseen interviewer, the man arrives carrying the pornographic magazine. He explains, "It's a souvenir." The interviewer observes, "You wrapped it in plastic." The man replies, "Yes, that way it won't get damaged. I like to keep souvenirs."

His keeping the magazine hints at the value that fetishists invest in inanimate objects that represent the elements of their fantasies. That he has wrapped it in plastic to preserve it from damage speaks of the fetishist's need both to protect the object (and the person it symbolizes) from his own destructiveness, and to control it by immobilization.

The woman focuses on the man's looks. His appearance deviates from her expectations. She says, "When I arrived, I knew it was him.

He was different from what I expected. But I wasn't disappointed."
She imagined him taller and asks how tall he is. She also wants to
know whether he is hairy. Her assertion that she was not disappointed
is the sort of negation that, classically, masks its opposite.

It is also of considerable interest that the author of the film,
Philippe Blasband, in a reversal of the status quo, assigned the perverse initiative to a woman. In spite of recent research into female
perversion, the overwhelming preponderance of clinical and empiri-
cal experience urges that sexual perversions, as we have come to
define them over a long taxonomic history, are, almost exclusively,
features of male behavior. This is especially so regarding fetishism.
What, then, are we to make of the author's choice, apart from its
novelty? One of its effects is to intensify the filmgoer's already strong,
and ultimately unsatisfied, curiosity about the nature of the perverse
act. A second might be to provoke further speculation regarding the
occult eros lurking within the eponymous "Dark Continent."

The perverse fantasy that the couple in the film intends to enact
requires a set of scripted sensory and behavioral elements, in opposition to a love relationship or other intimate friendship. The other
person's deviation from these requirements necessitates a species of
adaptation that may take several forms: the perverse individual can
fill the gap with private fantasy even while exhibiting no overt perverse behavior. S(he) can try to "teach" the other to approximate more
closely to the ideal perverse partner in her (his) particular fantasy;
s(he) can remain in the relationship with the less-than-perfect partner
while seeking more suitable ones; s(he) can sever the relationship and
go on with the quest for a better equipped partner.

But, parallel to all of these stratagems, there remains another
option. The couple may adapt to the deviation of their expectations
from the perverse ideal by initiating a relationship. By this I mean that
they might get to know one another by refocusing some of the attention originally fixed on perverse requirements on qualities unrelated
to the perverse scenario. That is, they may accept what is there, and,
to a greater or lesser degree, renounce the qualities they were hoping
to find. Such a displacement can only be affected where ego strength
is sufficient for delay, and where anxiety is controlled enough to
reduce the urgency for frequent release of tension through action.

The couple in the film, despite their preconceptions and their
fetishistic focus on body characteristics, begin, early on, to pay

attention to each other's faces. Robert Stoller, in his book *Sexual Excitement, Dynamics of Erotic Life* (1979, p. 8) wrote,

> The creation of a fetish, then is made up of several processes . . . The object is stripped of its humanity. This is easier to do with breasts, buttocks, legs, and penises than with faces. We reside in our faces. It takes more work to annihilate the person in the face.

The woman tells the interviewer, "He was smiling. He has a lovely smile. His eyes crinkle up and his whole face seems to smile. He's handsome when he smiles."

The man says, "I like real women. I found her attractive on her photo. Identity photos aren't flattering . . . don't know . . . She had something. Her expression held something special."

Thus, their humanizing consideration of each others' faces acts to subvert their initially pornographic purposes. The film's overture, then, introduces the themes of fetishistic needs with their necessary emphasis on isolated physical characteristics; the partial disappointment of these needs, and the consequent partial displacement of focus to the whole person, as reflected in the face.

The deviation from the fetishistic ideal is not the only obstacle to the successful acting out of the perverse fantasy. Another is the effect of time and space, which conduces to the diminution of infantile omnipotence by creating an awareness of the inevitability of absence and loss. It is instructive, in this regard, that the woman is upset when the man orders a drink at their first meeting in the bar. She wants no time to elapse before they repair to the hotel room to begin the scenario. Later on, the specter of loss and separation becomes even more prominent when the man pursues the woman into the Metro, driven by the fear that he might never see her again. Likewise, there are moments when each partner is made to endure a painful wait until the other finally appears.

The woman's wish to abrogate time and space is clearly expressed when she declares, "In fact, we should have met in a hotel room and never speak even outside." The hotel corridors are red, but the room in which they carry out their assignation is blue, signifying the subordination of passion to the cool and calculated protocol of the perversion. The man says, "We left the hotel as quickly as possible. We didn't feel guilty. We just wanted to be out in the open," underscoring the sense in which the confines of the hotel room represent a barrier rather than a boundary. The latter implies a zone across which transactions can occur; the former, a rigid obstacle to prevent engagement. Thus, the physical characteristics of the hotel symbolize splitting, which is endemic to perverse practice, and designed fundamentally to negate certain unbearable aspects of reality.

Throughout the film, other people are frequently interposed between the two principal characters, and there is almost always a third person either intruding or threatening to intrude on their privacy. For example, there are the ubiquitous chambermaid and her cart, the room clerk, people on the street and in bars, the unseen interviewer, and, most dramatically, the elderly man who interrupts their lovemaking by trying his key in the lock of their room, and then by suffering a heart attack in the corridor. If the awareness of time and space opposes the purposes of perversion, the perceived intrusion of an additional person or persons, is the *coup de grâce*. The man who suffers a heart attack epitomizes the event that diverts their aims most decisively, first, because it galvanizes humane and compassionate responses from them, behavior that is at odds with the necessary ruthlessness of perverse culture. Second, because it coerces them to collaborate in a helpful and purposive way. Third, because it involves them, willy-nilly with the man's wife and the complications of her relation to her husband. Fourth, and most important, because it introduces the specter of death, the ultimate reality that perversions are designed to deny.

For it will be seen that perversion is, first and foremost, a moratorium on the claims of reality, especially those deriving from separation and loss. It differs from such kindred phenomena as play and improvisation by being rigidly exclusionary. One couples theorist (Dr. Albert Brok, 2006), posits that a successful relationship must include an element of risk or unpredictability within a safe perimeter, but the boundary must be sufficiently permeable to permit the introduction of novel experience. In the perversion, the barrier is designed to ward off novelty so that the essence of fantasy remains impervious to change. Where, in play, a person may accept illusion without losing touch with reality, in perversion, the basic objective is not the acceptance of an illusion under the sanction of reality, but rather insistence that the illusion *is* reality. This insistence is supported by the banishment of any competing claims.

*   *   *

Our film couple, then, have met for the purpose of playing out a perverse fantasy; have encountered impediments to doing so, first in each person's falling short of the other's perverse ideal; next, in the logistical difficulties of time and space; finally in the intrusion into their private space by other people. They respond to these problems by attempting to alter the basis of their relationship from perverse to romantic. For a while, they are optimistic over the prospect of their mutual continuity and development but, unable to sustain their hopefulness, project their doubts and misgivings into each other and separate.

Brok (2006, p. 9), comments on these events as follows:

> What defined their connection (and attachment) remains a shared experience protected from the intrusion of outside others. A secret without context . . . a couple without extension, a pair without involvement, a relationship organized by desire, but not by love.

I think it is of the essence that we understand what could be so special as to require such secrecy and protection. It would be easy enough to attribute the couple's failed efforts at closeness to insufficient maturity. But that would be to ignore, or trivialize, the importance of their initial project. The film dramatizes and forces us to attend to this question through the characters' adamant refusal to divulge the nature of their perverse scenario. Once, at the beginning of the film, and once at the end, the interviewer asks what the couple actually did in the hotel room. Both times, he is soundly rebuffed. Here are the words by which they refuse: The man says,

> No, no. Even if you tortured me, blinded me, strapped electrodes to my testicles, no. I'd rather die first.

The woman:

> Who the hell cares what it was. It could be anything. Yet it was always the same thing. It was an act of love. Even if it was special, even if people don't understand, even if they find it sick . . . even if it was purely sexual at first—that's what it was, all the same, an act of love.

Clearly the purpose for which the couple first met was to share an experience that each felt was highly significant and yet never before enacted by either of them. To have attained their adult status and yet never to have done this thing suggests that it carries meanings that are fraught and problematic. There are human beings whose perverse sexuality gains expression early in their lives, despite any accompanying sense of shame or guilt. But this couple waited a long time before deciding to act. Perhaps their drive was relatively weak, but it is more likely that they were sufficiently mature to conduct their sex lives along conventional lines even while harboring their perverse fantasies in some private recess of their inner lives and hoping, some day, to act on them. One can assume that their wish to do so had to overcome formidable resistance.

So, what does the perversion contain, and what does acting on it achieve that is so vital as to induce a couple otherwise capable of the kind of sexuality that we would assign to the genital stage, to take the risks necessary to carry it out behaviorally? Stoller (1979, p. 60), whose work I have already quoted, wrote,

> . . . it is hostility—the desire, overt or hidden, to harm another person—that generates and enhances sexual excitement. The absence of hostility leads to sexual indifference and boredom. The hostility of erotism is an attempt, repeated over and over, to undo childhood traumas and frustrations that threatened the development of one's masculinity or femininity. The same dynamics, though in different mixes and degrees, are found in almost everyone, those labelled perverse, and those not so labeled.

Although agreeing in principle with this formulation, I would suggest a more generalized application: that in the absence of a channel for the enactment of aggression in the sexual and nonsexual practices of couples whose relations to one another can be described as tender, empathic, compassionate, romantic, loving, or mature, their intimate lives together will lack excitement and vitality.

One of the essential goals of fetishization is to render the object indestructible and unburdened by personal needs, and, therefore, impervious to the depredations of aggressive attacks. Although this is an effective way of managing aggression, it may be difficult to reconcile with a perception of the other in which vulnerability, mutability, aging, and eventual loss, are essential features.

* * *

The use of an unseen interviewer to draw out the opinions, impressions, and retrospective feelings of the couple is somewhat jarring. It creates a second level of experience that has psychotherapeutic as well as journalistic overtones. Though the interviewer's role may be disguised by either of these, as well as others (e.g., a researcher in the mold of Kinsey or Masters and Johnson), his principal function is as a representative of our own curiosity regarding the hidden aspects of the couple's behavior and motives. At the manifest level of this task, he is a failure in the sense that the major factual mysteries remain unsolved. Latently, however, this device elicits responses from the two characters that deepen and enrich our understanding. But the interviews also make the point that the concrete facts are of far less importance than the power this film exerts in provoking thought on the nature of perversion and its relation both to sexuality and romantic love.

Certified Copy: The problem of verisimilitude

This essay, in lieu of being an explication, consists of a number of general reflections that may elucidate the film without addressing its particularities. I have chosen to elaborate on ideas provoked by the central ambiguity of the story in preference to treating its characters and action in any direct way. My rationale for this is partly that it seemed consistent with the intentions of the film-maker, and partly that it allowed me to explore some indigenously psychoanalytic ramifications of the material.

The notion advanced in the film, as the theme of James Miller's book, is, "Forget the original; just get a good copy." This theme bears on the psychoanalytic concept of transference, which may be defined as a copy, the original being the child's experience of his first objects, principally the one who assumes the position of mother, and her unique rendition of that role. It is often assumed that an optimal experience with the original will serve as a template for the copies that follow. That is, if the child experiences his objects as good enough, he will be motivated to seek others in later life who resemble them.

It has also been put forth that if the child experiences them as not good enough, or too frustrating, s(he) will be motivated to seek another in the same mold, in order to correct the "defects" in the original.

Another proposition has it that if the object is sufficiently good the child will be proportionately free of the need to find in the other resemblances to the original. Yet a fourth proposition is that if the object is too frustrating, the child will be motivated to renounce the original in favor of a totally different, more potentially gratifying, copy.

These may be condensed into three schematic transference configurations that are a function of the degree to which the dyadic and subsequent relations in a child's life have been satisfactory or unsatisfactory.

1. Where they have been radically unsatisfactory, it is often the case that, as a grownup, the person seeks relations with people who either resemble the original object, or can be made to do so by various stratagems. This transference is characterized by attempts to render the copy as much like the original as possible, and then to "perfect" this simulacrum by changing it to order; that is, to alter it to what the subject wanted it to be. These operations are conducted under the pressure of the repetition compulsion, and largely unconsciously.

2. A second possible outcome, where the originals have been radically unsatisfactory, is to seek relations with people who in no way resemble the original object, or can be made not to by various stratagems. This transference is characterized by attempts to render the copy as incompatible with, and different from, the original as possible. These maneuvers may prove futile with the passage of time, through the agency of the repetition compulsion and the return of the repressed.

3. Where the original relations were predominantly satisfactory, the person will be free to seek relations with someone whose qualities and features may or may not resemble those of the originals because judgment will be a function of clearer, less driven perception and thus directed to "real" characteristics of the other rather than to traits that lend themselves to positive or negative typecasting.

In the first two cases, because the original cannot be renounced, the person is strongly inclined to revert to copies. In the third case, the possibility of renouncing the original allows the person to relate to new originals.

* * *

The work of art that uses a percept as a point of departure is always an original because it is a selection and arrangement of the percept as well as subject to the idiosyncratic transformations of the artist's apperception. Added to these are the requirements of form, the most obvious and prevalent of which, in visual art, is the frame. Even a deliberate forgery can be detected precisely by the ways in which the aforementioned elements intrude, unbidden, into the counterfeiting process. Thus, even a deliberate forgery is, technically, an original. The exceptions are editions of graphic art and photography, where the original is a template designed to generate copies.

> Perhaps identity was not a building for which one had to find foundations, but rather a series of impersonations held together by a central intelligence that knew the history of the impersonations and eliminated the distraction between action and acting. (St. Aubyn, 2012, p. 70)

Additional materials that may have a bearing on the film and the psychoanalytic ideas connected with it are a poem by Edwin Arlington Robinson (1950, p. 129) titled "John Gorham" (see below); the thought experiment proposed by Erwin Schrodinger (1935, pp. 807–812), known as Schrodinger's Cat, in which a vial of poison and a source of deadly radiation are put into a box with a cat. If a geiger counter, also put in the box, detected radiation, the vial would be broken and the poison in it would kill the cat. Quantum mechanics predicts that the cat would be simultaneously dead and alive. If we were able to see into the box, however, we would learn that the cat was either dead or alive, but not both.

Applying this fancy to the film, we are forced to conclude that the man and the woman are, at the same time, married and not married. It should be noted, though, that Schrodinger, himself ran afoul of the codes of propriety of the various prestigious institutions of higher learning that offered him exceedingly lucrative positions when he insisted on maintaining a *ménage* that consisted of himself, his wife, and his mistress. Apparently, his belief that he was married, not married, and neither, was unacceptable to the people who were otherwise dazzled by his prodigious scientific and mathematical talent.

A third, possibly relevant, thought comes from the set of experiments conducted on the campus of Stanford University in 1971. Philip

Zimbardo (1971) and his research assistants assigned student volunteers randomly to the roles of prisoners and guards in a mock prison situation. Before long, both groups began to enact the requirements of these roles, to an alarming and dangerous degree. Perhaps what begins as a harmless game in the film eventuates in a situation where the role envelops the person and, moment by moment, inexorably deprives both participants of the aesthetic distance necessary to the exercise of freedom. If so, this says much for the power of roles, and takes us back to the passage from St. Aubyn.

Here is the poem I mentioned before. In it, a couple engages in what appears to be the terminal argument of their relationship. You may see some similarity between what they say to each other and some of the dialogue spoken by the couple in the film.

"Tell me what you're doing over here, John Gorham,
Sighing hard and seeming to be sorry when you're not;
Make me laugh or let me go now, for long faces in the moonlight
Are a sign for me to say again a word that you forgot."—

I'm over here to tell you what the moon already
May have said or maybe shouted ever since a year ago;
I'm over here to tell you what you are, Jane Wayland,
And to make you rather sorry, I should say, for being so."—

"Tell me what you're saying to me now, John Gorham,
Or you'll never see as much of me as ribbons any more;
I'll vanish in as many ways as I have toes and fingers,
And you'll not follow far for one where flocks have been before."—

"I'm sorry now you never saw the flocks, Jane Wayland,
But you're the one to make of them as many as you need.
And then about the vanishing. It's I who mean to vanish;
And when I'm here no longer you'll be done with me indeed."—

"That's a way to tell me what I am, John Gorham!
How am I to know myself until I make you smile?
Try to look as if the moon were making faces at you,
And a little more as if you meant to stay a little while."—

"You are what it is that over rose-blown gardens
Make a pretty flutter for a season in the sun;

You are what it is that with a mouse, Jane Wayland,
Catches him and lets him go and eats him up for fun."—

"Sure I never took you for a mouse, John Gorham;
All you say is easy, but so far from being true
That I wish you wouldn't ever be again the one to think so;
For it isn't cats and butterflies that I would be to you."—

"All your little animals are in one picture—
One I've had before me since a year ago to-night;
And the picture where they live will be of you, Jane Wayland,
Till you find a way to kill them or to keep them out of sight."—

"Won't you ever see me as I am, John Gorham,
Leaving out the foolishness and all I never meant?
Somewhere in me there's a woman, if you know the way to find her.
Will you like me any better if I prove it and repent?"—

I doubt if I shall ever have the time, Jane Wayland;
And I dare say all this moonlight lying round us might as well
Fall for nothing on the shards of broken urns that are forgotten,
As on two that have no longer much of anything to tell."
                                                    (Robinson, 1950, p. 129)

One implication of the poem is that something obtrudes between two people who care deeply about each other that is fatal to their union. Perhaps it is related to conflicting and mutually corrosive expectations that emanate from transference, or perhaps it stems from some more fundamental discontinuity between male and female natures. It may be that the model of interminable (or terminal) marriage that is held to be normative is inconsistent with the experience of a large and ever increasing number of couples. The relationship in this film seems to evolve from its inception to its ending in a pattern reminiscent of the structure classically ascribed to, or superimposed on, narrative. This involves some variant on an arch, with an inciting event, action developing to a climax, and then receding to a denouement.

The implication is that relationships have a natural history that, when played out, will lead to an inevitable ending. Such a model would derive from the transference schemata to which I have referred, rather than from any *a priori* ideal of lifelong partnership. Or, perhaps it is the tension between what people feel capable of, on the one hand, and what they aspire to, on the other, which lends special poignancy, pain, and gratification to seeing a film that is a love story. It will not go unnoticed that the woman most often aspires to interminable monogamy, whereas the man typically favors serial monogamy. The variations of this expectation are what render the narrative exciting: the flirtations, extra-dyadic affairs, oscillation of closeness and distance, alienation and reconciliation; who does what to and with whom. Always, however, these are departures, implicit or explicit, from the two basic themes.

Thus, the admonition to "Forget the original; just get a good copy," bears in myriad ways on the problematics of intimate linking. It can be interpreted as applying either to a particular person or kind of person, or to a relational format such as monogamy (continuous or serial), promiscuity, or even more complex variants. It can be regarded as a rationalization for the incapacity for constancy, an empirically arrived at truth, a self-consolation, or an attempt to persuade one's partner that one is at least as desirable as the original, if not more so.

Whether or not we accept the protagonist's advice will depend less on our ideologies than on our emotional responses to the film, because the advice itself is nothing more than a rhetorical element in a work of art. When we step beyond its boundaries, the questions I have been exploring enter a wholly different context.

Talk to Her: Love among the ruins

In the film *Talk To Her*, Benigno, a male nurse, acquires total responsibility for the care of a young dancer with whom he became infatuated prior to the accident that has left her in a coma. During the first few minutes of the film, he relieves the female nurse with whom he shared that responsibility of her duties, under the guise of allowing her to spend time with her children. Given his patient's comatose condition, and the absence of other caretakers to whom he might have to account for what he does, Benigno has, in addition to complete responsibility for her, complete control over her. He is free to verbalize and play out his fantasies without concern for the critical or corrective scrutiny of other people. The eponymous phrase, "Talk to her," refers to the monologue carried on by Benigno as he engages in an imaginary relationship with his patient, Alicia, while he also does things to her. What he does is care for her body in the most thoroughly intimate way.

The rationale for these ministrations is impeccable from the perspective of good nursing, but their underlying meaning is far removed from the domain of nursing, deriving rather from Benigno's psychopathology. Explaining his method to Marco, the film's other male protagonist, he says, "You have to pay attention to women, talk to them, be thoughtful occasionally, caress them, remember they exist, they're alive, and they matter to us. That's the only therapy. I know from experience."

Three times, before receiving an answer, Marco iterates, "What experiences have you had with women?" Benigno replies, "Me? A lot. I lived twenty years, day and night, with one, and four years with this one." The twenty years refers to the peculiar circumstances of his childhood, which he spent ministering to his mother in much the same fashion as to Alicia. From the account he gives to the psychiatrist whom he consults, it appears that his father abandoned his mother, a profoundly narcissistic woman, leaving her in a paralytic depression. Her son seemed to have devoted himself exclusively to her care, acquiring along the way training as a nurse and beautician to make his work with her more effective. It can be inferred that the main reason for his total devotion to the care of his mother was that, without it, she would have become utterly lost to him. As we observe his treatment of Alicia, we are able to conclude that his very survival depended on his ability to create a mother by applying his imagination to the pliant raw material of her mere physical presence.

This, then, is Benigno's principal model for an intimate relationship. In the first instance, it requires denial of the truth that the woman is unavailable to him; next, the fabrication of her person from wishes superimposed upon the surviving fragments of a lost reality; then, an engagement, both verbal and physical, with the entity he has thus created; finally, in a critical boundary violation, yielding to his forbidden unconscious wishes as they press for release in action.

Though there is an unmistakably oedipal component to these wishes, their pregenital origins are far more significant. It will be recalled that the rape by which Benigno impregnates Alicia occurs after he has seen a silent film that profoundly disturbed him. The film is about a man named Alberto, who is radically reduced in size as a result of having drunk an elixir synthesized by his lover, Amparo, a research chemist. Prior to this transformation, Amparo accuses Alberto of selfishness. To refute this charge, he takes it upon himself to be the first experimental subject to test her newly discovered substance. Immediately after swallowing the potion, he kisses Amparo, who says, "It's done wonders for you."

Presumably, it has eliminated his selfishness. The selfishness refers to the kind of egocentricity that is typical of a child. By agreeing to imbibe this chemical, Alberto is renouncing his egocentricity and the self of which *selfishness* is the prime manifestation in favor of a return to the state of primary identification, a re-fusion with the mother that is literal and somatic. For, as we see in the film-within-a-film, after his reduction in size, he spends years in the home of his mother, who is described as "terrible," until he is rescued by Amparo, with whom he merges by entering her body through her vagina while she is asleep.

What is so disturbing about the film for Benigno is that it echoes the story of his own life and resonates with the unconscious fantasies that contain the solutions to the problems that cause his suffering. Using what we learn about his history at various points in the film, we may infer that, prior to his father's leaving his mother, he had begun to individuate, to differentiate himself from his mother as a separate entity. When his mother reacted to the loss of his father so calamitously as to withdraw from all affective contact with her child, however, he was forced into a regression from incipient selfhood back to primary identification, a process of de-differentiation.

In order to effect this, however, he needed to resuscitate her or at least keep her sufficiently alive to sustain his hopes of becoming one with her. This he did by taking care of her body and talking to her as though she were engaged in a relationship with him—that is, by speaking to her and inventing her answers. To put it more technically, he became her ego functions: a caretaker and a voice. Two months after his mother died, he initiated a relationship with Alicia, with whom he had become infatuated as a result of observing her from the window of his apartment. She was to be his Amparo, the good mother by which he hoped to repair the damage done him by his biological (bad) mother's abandonment. But the kind of relationship he has in mind is foreshadowed by his invasion of her living space following his consultation with her father. He imbibes her milieu with his eyes, taking in the artifacts and furnishings of her room as, later, he will appropriate her activities and interests. Next, he touches her things—the toy truck that he nudges from the shelf and then replaces, and the toy acrobat that he flips upward; finally, he takes something—not anything he has already touched, for these are too developmentally advanced for his purposes—a plastic hair clip resembling a set of sharp, interlocking teeth that symbolizes the primitive oral greed provoked in him by Alicia and her belongings. This impulse to devour the envied object is the sadistic counterpart of the passive wish to be enclosed and disappear into her.

Benigno struggles with these alternatives throughout the film. In the light of this struggle, his decisive act of raping the comatose Alicia can be seen as a condensation of the two warring inclinations. He invades her body, but also deposits a simulacrum of himself within her, in fantasy, a homunculus Benigo who will either never again emerge, like Alberto, or be reborn as a child whose mother can love him and help him to grow.

When Alicia evinces shock and alarm at discovering Benigno in her room, he assures her, "I'm harmless," an asseveration that seems supported by his name, which means benign. As we have already seen, however, his benignity consists chiefly of the ability to sublimate and keep in check his destructive impulses most of the time. If Benigno has a forerunner and counterpart in the history of film, it would be Norman Bates, the protagonist of Hitchcock's *Psycho* (1960). Their dynamics are similar except that Norman becomes his destructive mother and murders her rivals, whereas Benigno's appropriation of his mother and her surrogates is by symbolic and literal acts of internalization.

It is important to note that this man, to whom talking is so essential, is influenced decisively by a silent film: perhaps this is meant to convey that his deepest, most trenchant, motives are preverbal. As we have seen, they consist of the need to rescue his mother from insensibility in order to fuse with her. This rescue is so crucial that he will go to any length to achieve it, and the extremity to which his efforts take him is the sacrifice of reality for the sake of an elaborate delusion.

*   *   *

Marco, Benigno's co-protagonist, is also a rescuer of women. In fact, the affinity between the two men is established in the opening sequence when, seated next to each other in a theater, they witness a dance performance in which two women, apparently sleep-walkers in danger of colliding with furniture as they move across the stage, have their paths cleared by a man with a sad face. Benigno looks at Marco and discerns that he is crying, a fact that he includes in the description of the performance that he gives to Alicia the following day. Though we cannot know it until later in the film, Marco identifies instantly with the sad-faced man, as one whose mission in life has been to rescue women from painful and dangerous situations. Benigno, in contrast, is unaware of his need to rescue women. Instead, he experiences a specious contentment in his delusional intimacy with Alicia.

Both Marco and Benigno fail, ultimately, to protect and rescue their women from destructive collisions, but the results of these failures differ radically. When Marco cannot prevent Lydia from being gored by a bull, she is lost to him forever, but when Benigno cannot prevent Alicia from being hit by a car, she becomes more accessible to him. Both women are shown to be suicidal. Lydia takes greater and greater risks in the bullring, until her goring becomes inevitable; Alicia is given to jaywalking that increases the likelihood of her being hit. That Lydia is trying to regain the love of the man who rejected her, as well as please and be reunited with her deceased father (a bullfighter's assistant) by her increasingly more dangerous maneuvers in the ring, seems clear. The motives of Alicia's risk-taking behavior are less clear, however, possibly consisting of an escape from the tyranny of her fanatical dancing teacher or of dance, itself, possibly youthful bravado and omnipotence.

The divergent outcomes of the two accidents underscore the basic differences between the personalities of the two protagonists. For Marco, Lydia's coma closes off their relationship; for Benigno, Alicia's coma opens the way to greater relational possibilities, albeit delusional ones. Marco seems in constant mourning for the lost object of his love. The mourning is made possible by his acknowledgement of the loss. Yet, it is also clear that he is fatally attracted to women who will reject him, as illustrated by how powerfully he is drawn to Lydia when he first sees her on the television screen. Later, in response to her asking whether he writes about bullfighting, he replies, "To be honest, I know nothing about it," to which she snaps, "So why are you here?" "I know nothing about bullfighting, but a lot about desperate women," is his answer. It is probable, then, that Marco suffered an early object loss that he is repetitively reliving in an attempt to resolve his mourning just as Benigno deals with his early loss by means of a delusional belief that it never occurred. Accordingly, the film juxtaposes a man in continuous mourning with a man incapable of mourning.

* * *

There are other conclusive and mutually illuminating comparisons between the two men: Benigno's life has been lived within a tight, suffocating circumference, with little experience beyond its borders. Marco is an outsider, a wanderer who travels for a living and is rarely still. Both, however, are lonely, and this is one of the attributes that draws them together. But the quality of their respective loneliness is quite different. Benigno poignantly describes his when, speaking to Marco about the Cubans he has written about in his guidebook, he says,

> I really identified with those people who've got nothing and invent everything. When you describe that Cuban woman leaning out a window by the 'Malecon' waiting uselessly, seeing how time passes and nothing happens, I thought that woman was me.

He says this, however, only after he has been jailed and can no longer use his relationship with Alicia to combat his loneliness. A short time earlier, he had described to Marco the bliss he had experienced with Alicia:

> I started going to the ballet on my days off and to the cinemathèque. I try to see all the silent movies, German, American, everything. Then I tell her all I've seen. These last four years have been the richest of my life, looking after Alicia, doing the things she liked to do except traveling, of course.

Marco describes his loneliness to Lydia in a conversation about the woman he used to love: "I'd cry when I saw something that moved me because I couldn't share it with her ... There's nothing worse than leaving someone you still love ... love is the saddest thing when it goes away." Again, and even more poignantly, his experience of loneliness is reflected in the words of the song, "Paloma" (Sosa, 1954), that is so masterfully rendered by Caetano Veloso:

They say that through the nights
He passed by them, crying.

They say he didn't sleep . . .
They swear that even the sky
Shook in hearing his lament,
How he suffered that even until death
He cried for her.

Cucurrucucu, he sang . . .
Dying in his mortal passion.

. . . they swore that the dove
Was nothing more than his soul
That still waits for
The return of his beloved.

Marco is so moved by the words and music that he must walk away from the performers, but his progress is arrested by a picket fence, a visual symbol of his inability to put the sadness far behind him. When Lydia catches up with him, he tells her "This song gives me goose bumps," and goes on to answer her question as to why he cried after killing the snake in her kitchen on the night they met. He explains, "Years ago, I had to kill another snake. We were in Africa. She had the same phobia as you. She was waiting outside the tent, terrified, defenseless, and totally naked." Marco recalls this episode while sitting in Lydia's hospital room late at night. The recollection verges into a dream from which he awakens with the sensation of Lydia's kiss on his lips. The reference to Angela's nakedness recalls an earlier scene in which Marco phones Lydia at her hotel the morning after the snake incident. He asks her "How are you?" She replies, "Naked," an unconscious betrayal of her vulnerability.

More relevant than the cliché that ascribes phallic significance to snakes is the relation between the snake in Lydia's house and the painful memories of her broken relationship with Nino De Valencia, which sting like a poisonous serpent. Her house is so infected with these agonizing memories that she cannot return to it. A second snake image, not so dramatic as the first, is a picture frame in the shape of a snake surrounding a photograph of Alicia. The framed photo is on the table next to Alicia's hospital bed, along with her lava lamp, and a book about the American movie, *Night of the Hunter* (Laughton & Mitchum, 1955), in which Robert Mitchum plays a murderous preacher on the fingers of whose hands are printed the words "love," and "hate," a hint, perhaps, at the elemental antinomies that underlie Benigno's fanatical devotion to the care of Alicia. Likewise, the photograph of Alicia, encircled by a snake, suggests the veiled toxicity and rapacity of his attachment.

Viewing these artifacts on the night table of a comatose woman, Marco is bewildered, although he says nothing, but it is Benigno's behavior that really repels him. He experiences it as freakish and unnatural. Only gradually does he become sufficiently inured to the disquieting ambience created by Benigno to begin a relationship with him. Since this relationship is one of the film's key elements, it is important to explore why, and how it develops.

* * *

Marco's first glimpse into Alicia's room occurs as he is on his way to speak with Lydia's doctor. Through the narrow space afforded by the slightly ajar door, his gaze is riveted by the sight of Alicia, naked but for a sheet across her pelvis in a pose reminiscent of Goya's "Naked Maja," or Manet's "Olympia." He nudges the door further open and, as he regards her, Alicia's eyes open in what seems like an answering stare. He is so shocked by this that he retreats precipitously to the office of Dr. Vega, whom he asks about Lydia's prognosis. The doctor offers no hope at all for Lydia's recovery, explaining that her cerebral cortex has been irreparably damaged. He then shows Marco a magazine article describing the miraculous recovery of a similarly comatose woman. Marco regards this disclosure as a very tenuous shred of hope despite the obvious difference between the two cases: the brain of the woman in the article was not damaged; Lydia's was "destroyed."

Returning from the doctor's office, he stops, again, in front of the partly open door to Alicia's room, and is noticed by Benigno, who invites him in. At first, he shies away, but returns to accept Benigno's invitation. Marco is clearly vulnerable at this point: he is not yet prepared to accept the finality that Lydia is lost to him, and there is something about the combination of Alicia's having opened her eyes moments before and the magazine article shown him by the doctor that provides a buffer against complete despair. For this reason, he is drawn back to Alicia's room, where, despite his initial repulsion, he is tempted to accept the validity of Benigno's tacit assumption that Alicia is sentient and receptive to communication. This, then, is the initial basis for their friendship: Benigno initiates Marco into a kind of *folie à deux* to strengthen his own belief, and Marco participates in order to ward off, for a time, the certainty that he has lost Lydia.

Once begun, however, their relationship takes on a momentum of its own. Marco, who cannot for long suppress the painful reality of loss, is intrigued by Benigno's capacity to use delusion as a bulwark against it. At the same time as he is appalled by it, he also appreciates the artistry that allows Benigno to finesse reality. In addition, there is something about the comfort and ease with which Benigno engages with Alicia's body that intrigues Marco. He, like the viewer of the film, is affected by it as by the "uncanny," as Freud (1919h) used the term to denote a once-familiar experience that, as a consequence of repression, has become strange and, therefore, somewhat frightening.

Benigno's attraction to Marco is driven initially by the hope of recruiting a man in a circumstance similar to his own, as a secret sharer or a proselyte to his own delusion. He is also curious about the reasons for Marco's tears when he sat beside him at the dance performance. There is something about Marco's sadness, sensitivity to loss, and easy access to affect that attracts Benigno. Perhaps he is reminded of his mother's depression and feels an urge to counteract Marco's.

Until Benigno is incarcerated, the motives of each of the men are more or less self-serving. Even after he is jailed, Benigno continues to use Marco chiefly as a source of information about Alicia. It is only when he despairs of ever learning about Alicia and the fetus she was carrying that his bond with Marco achieves a different level. At this point, his love for Marco becomes unconditional, an end in itself rather than a means to other ends. For his own part, Marco is able to overcome the slavish adherence to reality that always prevented him from suspending his disbelief in Benigno's delusion to a sufficient degree to "talk to him," at his graveside.

Thus, each undergoes a vital transformation as a result of his experience with the other. No matter how briefly or tenuously, Benigno is able to love a real person rather than a delusional creation, and Marco is able, no matter how provisionally, to accept the validity of that which can only be imagined. The changes are believable within the indigenous premises of the film. Their modest proportions prevent their straining our credulity and their emotional impact is the greater for it.

*   *   *

Last, and perhaps most weighty among the myriad questions raised by *Talk to Her* that can be addressed within the limits of a relatively short essay is, why—after four years of homeostasis—does Benigno begin to test the limits of his role with Alicia, eventually violating the critical boundary between what is permissible and what is forbidden? Part of the answer lies in opportunity. Matilde, the nurse with whom he shares Alicia's care is a single mother whose child-care arrangements have been derailed; she is needed at home and can no longer nurse Alicia. Rather than risk the possibility of her being replaced by another nurse, Benigno volunteers to take her shifts as well as his own. By so doing, he is helping a woman whose husband abandoned her, as his father abandoned his mother. But even more meaningfully, he is also contriving to be Alicia's sole caretaker, a circumstance that allows full expression to his possessiveness and fantasy life. On the night during which he impregnates Alicia, Rosa, another nurse who sometimes assists him, is out with the flu. Thus, there is no one, no other nurse, nor Alicia herself, to whom he must account for his behavior. Alicia's only other regular visitor, Katerina, her dance teacher, also leaves on an extended assignment in Geneva. It is significant that, immediately after her departure from her last visit, Benigno outlines his plans for redecorating his apartment according to the designs illustrated in a home magazine. The clear implication is that these changes are in preparation for having Alicia live with him. This is made explicit when he divulges to Marco his intention to marry Alicia.

Having cleared all other obstacles from his path to Alicia, Benigno must come to terms with the final impediment—his own superego. His efforts to do so are augmented by the impact of the silent film that vibrates so sympathetically with his unconscious fantasy as to overcome any remaining inhibitions.

It is instructive to compare Benigno's relations to Alicia with a patient's relation to an analyst. The inherent similarity is that both are encouraged to talk: the patient by the analyst's initial instructions and subsequent silences, Benigno's by his own need to speak, as well as by Alicia's silent presence. The obvious difference is that the analyst is presumed to be awake and listening (though some analysands would dispute this), whereas Alicia is comatose. The analyst's alertness and awareness may be attested by her (his) interpretations and non-verbal responses, whereas Benigno's belief that Alicia can hear and understand him can be verified, if at all, only if she emerges from her coma.

Both sets of conditions are optimal for the evocation and proliferation of transference. Both are situations in which discourse can be pursued in a relatively uninterrupted way, which is why it can arrive at destinations that are unreachable in an ordinary dialogue. That is, the relative absence of cuing from the other makes it possible for the speaker to project aspects of her (his) inner world onto the other and, thus, engage in a progressively more inner-determined dialogue between self and object(s). In psychoanalysis, this dialogue is necessarily interrupted by any intervention of the analyst's, to a lesser or greater degree, depending on how much of the analyst's personal presence is manifest in his or her intervention. The latter, in turn, is a function of the analyst's judgment regarding the degree of her (his) personal presence that the patient needs at the moment, combined with his (her) own largely unconscious need to feel present, personally.

Lewin (1955, pp. 169–199) suggested that, in his (her) interpretative function, the analyst is comparable to the father who awakens the child from a dream. This perspective is consonant with the idea that transference is a regression that must be curtailed from time to time in order to allow the analytic process to achieve its ultimate goal, the diminution of transference and the establishment, in its place, of a way of engaging with oneself and the world that is deemed to be more consistent with what *is* rather than what is *wished for.*

It is in this that Benigno's talking diverges most from that of an analytic patient. In the absence of a responsive partner to his discourse, it regresses from the implicit wishes expressed in his *talk to her* to explicit gratification. In comparison, the one instance in which Marco takes the risk of talking without allowing for a response from Lydia prevents her from telling him that she plans to break off with him and return to Nino De Valencia, with whom she is still in love. This is another example of the disastrous effect of only *talking*, but not *listening*, to her. In his combined twenty-four years of experience with women, Benigno has done all the talking. I think that even Freud, who confessed that he did not know what women want, would have agreed that, on balance, they prefer being listened to to being talked to.

* * *

The film ends as it began, at a dance performance. This one is attended by Alicia, Katerina, and Marco. During the intermission, Alicia and Marco speak briefly to each other. The implication is that they will begin a relationship. That it will not be without its difficulties is suggested by Katerina's response to Marco's predicting, when they speak, that, "It will be simpler than you think;" she says, "Nothing is simple. I'm a ballet mistress and nothing is simple."

Prior to the intermission, the onstage action consists of a female dancer's being conveyed on a wave formed by the arms of several supine male dancers until she is raised and held by two standing male dancers. She is moved about by these men while singing a ballad into a microphone. The words to the song (Bausch, 1998) approximate to Alicia's recent experiences:

> Made love last night:
> It wasn't good; it wasn't bad.
> Intimate strangers . . .
> When I woke up this morning . . .
> It slowly dawned on me
> That my baby was gone.

She is held upright for a few seconds before she falls forward into the arms of men who catch her. She was made love to during the literal night, which stands, as well, for the long night of her coma. When she awakens from it, she has lost her baby.

The mood of the performance that follows the intermission is literally and figuratively upbeat, in stark contrast to the more somber tone of its predecessor. Couples in colorful costumes, the women barefoot and with their backs to the audience, emerge from one of the wings and dance across the stage to a Latin rhythm. The women shake their bottoms suggestively, in unison, to the beat. The line dissolves; one couple remains on stage, the man with his back to the audience, facing the woman. They are engaged in a bucolic mating ritual. Streams of water, signifying renewal, spring from the foliage behind them. There is an uncharacteristic, and for that reason, radiant smile on Marco's face. As he turns to look back at Alicia, seated two rows behind him, a printed caption announces "Marco and Alicia." Between them, there is an empty seat, representing Benigno. When Marco turns back to the stage, his face, and that of Alicia are aglow with reflected light, in contrast to the more naturally lit faces of all other members of the audience.

Talk to Her, a film constructed of parallels and symmetries, begins and ends with a dance performance. That which opens the film is about two sleepwalking women; the one with which the film ends is about an awakening. Between them stretches a sequence of events in which two of the four principal characters die, Lydia as a result of taking suicidal risks and Benigno by an actual suicide. Sometimes Death defeats Eros; sometimes Eros takes the lead. No matter what eventually happens between Alicia and Marco, their relationship will always be deeply informed by those whom they have lost.

Gods and Monsters: "Gaiety transfiguring all that dread"

The title of this section is quoted from a poem titled "Lapis Lazuli", by William Butler Yeats. I quote the passage in which it appears to establish the context:

> All perform their tragic play,
> There struts Hamlet, there is Lear,
> That's Ophelia, that Cordelia;
> Yet they, should the last scene be there,
> The great stage curtain about to drop,
> If worthy their prominent part in the play,
> Do not break up their lines to weep.
> They know that Hamlet and Lear are gay;
> Gaiety transfiguring all that dread.
> Black out; Heaven blazing into the head:
> Tragedy wrought to its uttermost.
> (1983d, pp. 187–188)

When Yeats wrote the poem, the word *gay* had not yet been pressed into its current use to denote homosexuality, and yet it is apropos in talking of *Gods and Monsters* since the film, to quote James Whale's characterization of *The Bride of Frankenstein*, is a comedy about death as well as the depiction of the relationship between a homosexual man and a heterosexual one. The "dread" is a function of the unprecedented violence and destructiveness of the First World War, the uncanny, disquieting workings of Whale's disordered brain, the monstrosities related to the monster, its creators and its creation, Boone's and the world's homophobia, and death, as the ubiquitous unknown. "Gaiety" refers to the film's wit and humor, its sly camp, its exploration of homosexuality, but most essentially to its implication that the best approach to the things that cause dread is the combination of creativity, laughter, and love divested of sentimentality. Finally, the middle term, "transfiguring," takes note of the innumerable metamorphoses related to themes such as the creation of monsters, the creation of films, altered states of consciousness, changes of external appearance, and emotional transformations.

Made in 1998, the film was directed by Bill Condon and written by Bill Condon and Christopher Bram, from whose 1995 novel, *Father of Frankenstein*, it was derived. Much of the factual material on which the novel (and, therefore, the film) was based is to be found in a biography of James Whale written by James Curtis in 1982, an expanded and updated edition of which was published in 1998 under the title, *James Whale: A New World of Gods and Monsters*. Sir Ian McKellen's portrayal of James Whale is, by any standard, a *tour de force*, but no small element of its brilliance is that it enhances rather than eclipses the performances of the other principals, Brendan Fraser and Lynn Redgrave.

The facts of Whale's life, as presented in the film, are substantially accurate.

The following information was gleaned from the Curtis (1998) biography. He was born in 1889 in the city of Dudley in the West Midlands of England, to a working class family. His father was an ironworker. James was the youngest of five children. The family lived in a slum. He drew and painted from an early age; studied at the Dudley School of Arts and Crafts until 1914; enlisted in the British army in 1915 after the First World War began; was trained as an officer; served with distinction in Flanders until 1917, when he and two others were taken prisoner by the Germans and interned in the POW camp Holzminden, where some of the prisoners occupied their time by producing plays to be performed by their comrades. Whale contributed by designing and painting scenery, acting, and participating in the writing of original material. When the war ended, he began his career as a theater professional, at first as a set designer and actor, then, by degrees, a stage manager and director. By the late 1920s, he had begun directing films in England and in 1930, he arrived in Hollywood to direct for Universal Studios. In 1931, he directed the original *Frankenstein*, in 1935, *The Bride of Frankenstein*, and, in 1936, incongruously, he directed *Show Boat*.

Around 1948, he retired from filmmaking: he traveled in Europe and did whatever pleased him. Whale suffered his first stroke in 1956, a relatively mild one, but a few months later was stricken with a second that was much more debilitating and for which he was hospitalized. On being discharged, he was cared for by a male nurse named William Jay Wrigley, an amiable, naïve and muscular young man who provided one part of the model for the character of Clay Boone, the other being Pierre Foegel, the chauffeur, companion, and lover whom he had acquired in France after his separation from David Lewis, his partner for twenty-two years.

On May 29, 1957, James Whale wrote the following note:

TO ALL I LOVE,

Do not grieve for me. My nerves are all shot and for the last year I have been in agony day and night—except when I sleep with sleeping pills—and any peace I have by day is when I am drugged by pills.

I have had a wonderful life but it is over and my nerves get worse and I am afraid they will have to take me away. So please forgive me, all those I love and may God forgive me too, but I cannot bear the agony and it [is] best for everyone this way.

The future is just old age and illness and pain. Goodbye all and thank you for all your love. I must have peace and this is the only way.

Jimmy

p.s.

Do not let my family come—my last wish is to be cremated so nobody will grieve over my grave. No one is to blame—I have wonderful friends and they do all they can for me, but my heart is in my mouth all the time and I have no peace. I cannot keep still and the future would be worse. My financial affairs are all in order and I hope will help my loved ones to forget a little. It will be a great shock but I pray they will be given the strength to come through and be happy for my release from this constant fear. I've tried hard all I know for a year and it gets worse inside, so please take comfort in knowing I will not suffer anymore.

J.

After sending the note in an envelope addressed "TO ALL I LOVE," he walked to the shallow end of his swimming pool and threw himself in head first, hitting his head against the bottom in the hope of knocking himself unconscious. When his maid, Anna Ryan, found him, he was dead.

Little is known or said about this maid, so it is unlikely that she was the model for Hanna in the film. Parenthetically, while Hanna is German or Hungarian, Maria, her counterpart in the novel, is Mexican.

The material of the film, then, is basically fact that is imaginatively augmented and enhanced. I think we can assume that there was something about the figure of James Whale that inspired this conception and that the film, therefore, captures some essence of Whale's life. In what follows, I shall try to elucidate this essence.

Unlike the novel, the film opens on Clay Boone, showing us his unceremonious toilette and breakfast: his day starts with a shave, a cigarette, and a beer. He is a bit of a brute. In contrast, his employer, James Whale, is an elegant man. But he has had a stroke that has left him prey to revivifications, hallucination-like experiences of past events that he can neither repress nor censor. We are reminded of the line from Freud's *Studies on Hysteria* (1895d, p. 6), "Hysterics suffer mainly from reminiscences." Whale describes this phenomenon as "an electrical storm." In *Frankenstein*, the monster is brought to life through the agency of an electrical storm and this parallel is further emphasized when, in a later conversation with Clay, Whale points to his head and exclaims, "The only monsters are here." Whale also suffers from a precipitous decline in all his functions. As a result, he wants to die. But he cannot take his own life; he must find someone to kill him, someone whom he can direct. He is, after all, a director, and wishes to direct his own death and to motivate his killer to a good performance. He needs to overcome his helplessness by asserting control over the end of his life, as a director controls the elements of a film. But it is this very helplessness that he also longs for: the fantasy of the monster carrying him to his death as Karloff does with Mae Clark in the original film is his underlying wish of being loved/consumed by his father. He sees Boone as a part-object, clay to be molded into the material of his fantasy (as Frankenstein saw the monster). Clay's entrance into his life is a boon to Whale, a gift from the powers that be, to help him carry out his plan.

In the encounter with Whale, however, something complex and sentient is awakened in Boone, and he begins to become a person. Reciprocally, Boone catalyzes critical reminiscences in Whale and there develops between them a kind of relational psychotherapy. The fictitious, semi-aristocratic persona that Whale used in his interview with the pretentious and shallow Mr. Kay is easily relinquished in response to Boone's ingenuousness. Whale says, "I've spent my whole life outrunning the past and now it floods all over me. There is something about the openness of your face that makes me want to tell the truth." Boone agrees to allow Whale to draw his picture. During the first sitting, Whale says he is interested in the architecture of Boone's head. We are instantly aware of the resemblance between it and that of the monster, but Boone becomes intrigued with his own head as a result of Whale's interest. This broaches a theme that is developed throughout the film of the peculiar relationship between the head and the rest of the body—for example, in Whale's dream, he is the monster and Boone is Henry Frankenstein replacing his brain; or earlier, in the neurologist's office, where Whale learns that his problem is "only above the neck." Watching *The Bride of Frankenstein* (1935) in the diner, Boone begins to appreciate complexity and to ask questions. He reads up on Whale, to whom he has begun to develop a troubling, yet important relationship. For the first time, it occurs to him that something can be funny and scary at the same time.

When Whale describes his childhood to Boone, he asserts, "I was a freak of nature," an ambiguous allusion to his artistic proclivities as well as to his homosexuality, both qualities that alienated him from family and community. In this, he resembles the monster with whom he identifies as an outcast, an alienated other. Recalling his feelings when making the pictures, he says to Boone, "But the monster never receives any of my jibes. He's noble—noble and misunderstood."

It is around this time that Whale hallucinates his father while looking at Boone. This leads to a discussion of his impoverished childhood and his father's antipathy to him. Boone responds with the recollection of his own father's unsympathetic and dismissive response to his being medically discharged from the Marine Corps. He had earlier protested, "Everyone's got stories to tell. Not me." But slowly he becomes able to reflect on his own life and to realize, through Whale's attentive kindness, that he does indeed have a story, albeit one that his shame had caused him heretofore to suppress. There is a rich irony in the juxtaposition of the tough, macho ex-marine who never got into a war, and the suave, effete homosexual who was a decorated hero of many battles. The comparison underscores the danger of stereotypy and raises serious questions regarding the true nature of manliness.

The most telling irony, however, is in the initial clash of assumptions on both sides, and the way they are eventually resolved. Whale assumes that Boone is a brute whose homophobia can be exploited into murder. Boone assumes that Whale is "an old fruit" who wants to seduce him. Neither can predict how their engagement will alter these assumptions: Boone, who starts out as all body, develops thought. Whale, who was a ruthless manipulator, a director, experiences love. Both begin their relationship with a stunted capacity for attachment, limited to part-object relations. The quasi-therapeutic conditions of their encounter engender growth and the ability to care about the other as an end rather than as a mere means.

That Whale wishes to die is an acceptable premise based on our understanding of his physical and mental suffering. But the manner of the death he wishes to arrange has far reaching psychodynamic implications. As I indicated earlier, he wishes to be killed by a figure akin to Frankenstein's monster as the fulfillment of a childhood wish to be loved/consumed by his father. There are hints both in his narrative and hallucinatory recollections of his childhood that he felt deprived of his father's love and approval and that this sense of rejection constituted a substrate upon which his war experiences, especially his relationship with Barnet, built the structure of his monster fantasy. This fantasy was given artistic expression in the two Frankenstein films, both of which supplied powerful symbolic imagery for the hallucinatory memories depicted in the film. Thus, the monster condenses an array of meanings including his father, himself as "a freak of nature," the horrendous destructiveness of the First World War, the abortive outcome of human omnipotence, and the personification of the way in which misunderstanding and persecution engender evil or aggression.

It was just after the First World War that Freud wrote *Beyond the Pleasure Principle* (1920g), in which he hypothesized the existence of a death instinct and a destructive compulsion to repeat painful experiences. Although the question of the origins of evil and destructiveness is not resolved in the film, there is the implication in the toast, "To a new age of gods and monsters," that humankind is endowed with both tendencies: they resemble gods in their creativity, beauty, and compassion, but also in their omnipotence, wantonness, and destructive power; they resemble monsters in their bestiality, rage, ugliness, and viciousness, but also in their vulnerability, tenderness, and victimization. These qualities are, by turns, illustrated in the content of

Whale's hallucinations where, alternately, Whale, Boone, and Barnet are transfigured into the monster who sometimes acts destructively and sometimes tenderly. They are rendered even more effective by being intercut with footage from the original Frankenstein films, most notably the scene between the monster and the blind hermit in which their cigar smoking echoes that of Whale and Boone over lunch. It is in this scene, too, that the fundamental antinomies with which Whale has struggled throughout his life are most clearly stated: the monster intones, "Love dead, hate living," and "Alone bad, friend good." Significantly, Whale is unconsciously in love with death, in fact literally so if Barnet can be seen as the incarnation of death. But his love of death predates the war and his only way of combatting it has been through comedy—the black comedy that had its origins in the trenches after he watched helplessly, day after day, Barnet's body disintegrating as it hung out of reach on barbed wire. He comments, "We were a witty lot, laughing at our dead, feeling that it was our death too but for each man—better you than me." Hence, though it was better to be alive, that life was attenuated by the guilt of the survivor and the yearning, illustrated in one of his hallucinations, to join Barnet and the others, for Barnet was a "friend" as no other had been or would be until he became involved with Clay Boone.

Just as Yeats supplied my title, so, too, did he anticipate the complex interplay of gods and monsters in his poem "The Second Coming" (Yeats, 1983a, pp. 187–188) where the paradoxical linkage of love and hate, peace and bloodshed, are symbolized by the idea that the Christian millennium featured a God of peace and love whose advent initiated 2000 years of war and bloodshed; the new millennium would feature a god who was a violent monster but consist of 2000 years of peace and love. Thus the lines:

> . . . but now I know
> that twenty centuries of stony sleep
> Were vexed to nightmare by a rocking cradle
> And what rough beast, its hour come round at last
> Slouches towards Bethlehem to be born.

The remarkable scene of George Cukor's party is another step in the exploration of human contradictions. It depicts polite society around a representative of the British royal family, a boring, pretentious, and hypocritical atmosphere to which Whale brings his gardener. They drive to the party in Whale's convertible with the top down, at Whale's request, a visual pun on the opening of the roof so that the monster may be exposed to the storm in *Frankenstein*. Predictably, a storm disrupts the party but not before a bizarre reunion takes place between Whale and his make-believe monsters. Here we see Boris Karloff, the original monster, as a devoted grand-uncle, doting on a child, and Elsa Lanchester, the make-believe bride, as a kindly, tactful old friend. The scene recalls an earlier one showing these principals on the set where *The Bride* is being made and there is banter about the cast's ambiguous sexuality. The innocuousness of the original monsters serves to highlight Whale's having assumed center stage in his own drama. When the storm breaks, it is he and Boone who are the principals in the fluid interplay between the monster and its creator that constitutes the film's *Gotterdammerung*—a twilight of the gods and monsters, the counterpart of the Wagnerian cataclysm.

When they arrive home, all through that night the storm continues to rage. The stage is now set for the enactment of Whale's farewell performance as a director, actor, and creator of a *mise-en-scène*. His lifelong romance with Thanatos is the theme; he is the god who creates and directs the scene, assumes omnipotent control over the events, and assigns the role of monster to Clay Boone. But Clay, having learned to love Whale, demonstrates some godlike qualities of his own. Agreeing to pose naked for Whale, he displays the body and demeanor of a Greek or Roman god to such a degree that Whale exclaims, "You're much too human," and conceives the notion of covering his face with the German gas mask. The god would then become a monster, a faceless brute of an enemy, blank and pitiless. Boone, however, refuses the role with the exclamation, "I am not your monster." Like others who, earlier in Whale's life have been so cast, Boone fails him. The failure consists of a rejection of the part-object function assigned to him, insisting instead, on being seen and treated as a whole person and earning this right with the gift of love rather than the gift of death for which Whale has ever longed. In the end, Whale's plan to create a monster whose embrace will bring death is thwarted: if Clay is not a monster, Whale cannot be a god; both are mere mortals but they are able to love and must accept this as their only redemption.

Essential to an understanding of Whale's personality is the fact that he has had three families over the course of his life: his family of origin, his *Frankenstein* family, and the final family consisting of himself, Boone, and Hannah. In all three cases, Whale can be considered the child of real or symbolic parents. In all three cases, the primary focus is on the father, the mother remaining in the background. I have already stated my assumption that Whale's longing for paternal love assumed the pathological form of a wish to be consumed to death and, thus, merged with his father. Fantasies of this kind are well explicated in a monograph titled *The Psychoanalysis of Elation* (1950), by Bertram Lewin. The fantasy was intensified by Whale's experiences as a soldier and later expressed in his *Frankenstein* films. The wish, at last, to act it out was potentiated by the devastating effects of his stroke, an event that both left him in pain and divested him of the control that he so valued and exercised in his career as a director.

Hannah, the mother in his third family, is a figure of greater significance than the earlier ones. Beneath her moralistic disapproval of his homosexual activities, she conceals a deep love and resentment of being excluded from the sphere of his erotic interests. This she displaces into a fierce protectiveness lest Whale's self-destructiveness result in his being harmed by his gay lovers. Her position in his household bears some resemblance to that of Mary Shelley, the author of the novel, *Frankenstein* (1992), on which the films were based. It was written in Switzerland, in a house that the Shelleys were sharing with Byron and two or three lesser figures of the Romantic Movement. On this particular evening, the group decided to engage in a competition by seeing who could write the best horror story. Those of the other contestants have not survived, but Mary Shelley's is the work that became *Frankenstein*. The book can be interpreted as a parable about womb envy—Victor Frankenstein's compulsion to create a human being. If he, and his collaborators, Dr. Pretorius, and Fritz, his lab assistant, were to succeed, they would have effectively excluded women from the process. Perhaps the story was precipitated by Mary Shelly's resentment of the inordinate degree of reciprocal interest of her husband and Byron, from which she felt excluded in much the same way as Hannah feels excluded. Whale does not need her to create his monster. Nevertheless, he loves her enough to reject the possibility of suicide by an overdose of medication, which he contemplates briefly early in the film. In the final irony of the film, she is able to implement her passion for him only after the death, for which he has yearned so deeply and so long, has already claimed him. It is after the drowning that she kisses him passionately on the lips.

Up to this point, the film's central tensions are only partially resolved. For example, we cannot assume that Whale's attachment to Boone or Boone's to Whale have wrought fundamental changes in the personality of either. True, they have had mutative experiences, but are these sufficient to have overcome the problems that were central to their psychic pain? The film, like the novel, could well have ended here but some irresistible Hollywood impulse required the neat coda in which we find Clay, apparently cured of his machismo and predilection for treating women as objects, happily married and the father of a son to whom, after a viewing of *Frankenstein* on television, he shows the drawing of the monster given him by Whale. As if this were not sufficient to convince us that he is a new man, he puts the boy to bed, wanders out into the misty rain, and, with the lights of home animating his face, plays at being a monster, just to show us that he is a whole person, not a caricature.

Nevertheless, this is an extraordinary movie in its serious and subtle treatment of the ways in which Thanatos merges with the more life affirming elements of experience to produce the ambiguities, paradoxes, and ironies that constitute the mysteries of the human condition.

In closing, I would like to quote the last section of Yeats' poem "Lapis Lazuli" because I think it conveys and illustrates the unique blend of tragedy and renewal that lies at the heart of *Gods and Monsters*. The poem was inspired by a seventieth birthday gift Yeats had received, a lapis lazuli carving dating to the eighteenth century depicting the scene that is described in this way:

> All things fall and are built again
> And those that build them again are gay.
>
> Two Chinamen, behind them a third,
> Are carved in lapis lazuli
> Over them flies a long-legged bird
> A symbol of longevity;
> The third, doubtless a serving-man,
> Carries a musical instrument.

Every discolouration of the stone,
Every accidental crack or dent
Seems a water-course or an avalanche,
Or lofty slope where it still snows
Though doubtless plum or cherry-branch
Sweetens the little half-way house
Those Chinamen climb towards, and I
Delight to imagine them seated there;
There, on the mountain and the sky,
On all the tragic scene they stare.
One asks for mournful melodies;
Accomplished fingers begin to play.
Their eyes mid many wrinkles, their eyes,
Their ancient, glittering eyes, are gay.

(1983d, pp. 187–188)

CHAPTER FOUR

Human identity

The encomiums to those we admire, particularly psychoanalysts, frequently emphasize their "humanity." Used often, and in widely diverse contexts, the word has been divested of a reliable set of connotations. It is usually intended to describe the ways and degrees to which the person bends or breaks rules or conventions in order to convey warmth or closeness to patients or supervisees. Accordingly, when we try to determine what is the essence of humanity, we are confounded by such tacit definitions as these.

The people who made the films I have placed in the category "Human identity" struggle to determine necessary and sufficient qualities that would qualify a creature for inclusion under that rubric. *Blade Runner* casts a net in which postmodern primates are caught along with Replicants, presumed to be machines. They are both mortal. That is, they will both die, the primates over the course of a human life expectancy, and the Replicants in four years. It is the condensed life span of the Replicants and their close kinship with their flesh and blood counterparts that render the essential tragedy of existence intelligible and meaningful.

What goes to make up the human is scrutinized in a different way in *Lord of the Flies*. In this film, we witness the gradual degradation of civilized inclinations to the point of barbarism. We cannot say, however, that the destructive behavior exhibited by the boys who become feral is less human than that of Ralph, who retains the decency into which he has been socialized. The conclusion to which we are forced is that to be human is as much to harbor murderous, sadistic, impulses, and to act on them, as it is to respond with tenderness, empathy, support, and lust to our fellow beings.

Seconds is a study of longing. There is a speech, discarded in the final cut of *Blade Runner*, in which Leon tries to explain the quintessence of the Replicant's condition. He says,

> Painful to live, isn't it? But that's how it is to be a slave. The future is sealed off. He grovels. He waits. Sex, reproduction, security, the simple things. But no way to satisfy them. To be homesick with no place to go. Potential with no way to use it . . . I tell you nothing is worse than having an itch you can never scratch. (Fancher & Peoples, 1980)

Ironically, Wilson, the protagonist of *Seconds*, a human, not a Replicant, suffers from the identical longing. The Replicants' fantasy that, given more time, they could find home, feel secure, and realize their potential, in sum, scratch the itch until it goes away, is given the lie in Wilson's experience. His purchase of more time in a younger body fails to satisfy his inchoate longing. The film suggests that we cannot fulfill our humanity quantitatively, even as it supports the notion that the wish to do so is also indigenously human.

In my discussion on *Blade Runner*, I invoke the neo-Platonist idea of the great chain of being, as revived in Arthur Lovejoy's (1972) eponymous study. It explores a hierarchical conception of being, with God at its apex and the inanimate at its base. Humans lie between the angels (and devils) at one extreme and beasts at the other. As a result, their natures are imbued with spiritual, moral, and compassionate qualities as well as sensual, brutal, and generally destructive ones. Human nature, therefore, tends to be more complex, adulterated, and variable than that of any other link in the great chain. This inconstancy is, of course, reflected in the three films in this category, but more significantly, it is the very tile and grout of dramatic art.

Blade Runner: The ghost in the machine*

Blade Runner, a film directed by Ridley Scott, was released to theaters in 1982. It was the forerunner of more recent film treatments of the relations between humans and androids such as *Artificial Intelligence* (Spielberg, 2001), and *Minority Report* (Spielberg, 2002). This juxtaposition is of particular interest to psychoanalysts because it stimulates thinking about what qualities are quintessentially human. By means of its rich symbolism and allusive cinematic vocabulary, the film explores such questions as the nature of the superego, the Oedipus complex, identity formation, and the eternal struggle between *Eros* and *Thanatos*. I use the material of the film to comment on some of the fundamental differences between Freud's world view and that of the neo-Freudians.

There is something deeply evocative about the phrase *Blade Runner*. It conjures manifold images along a spectrum from skating to stabbing but its specific relation to the characters and incidents of this film is by no means obvious. What, then, does the compound noun *Blade Runner* evoke, and how can we understand its function as a title, aware that titles have to embody some essence of the work? To me, it suggests a person trying to negotiate the sharp edge of a knife at great speed: metaphorically, someone for whom every step of everyday life is fraught with myriad dangers. I think of Rick Deckard trying to refuse Captain Bryant's directive to resume his bounty hunting and Bryant's brutal reply, "You know the score pal. If you're not a cop, you're little people" (Silverman, n.d.). Whichever alternative he chooses, he cannot get off the blade, and, if this is true for Deckard, it is just as true for the other characters, because *Blade Runner*, though set in the future and based on a technological premise, belongs irrefutably to the genre of *film noir*.

One definition of *film noir* (Dirks, 1996–2002, para. 1), states,

> The primary moods of classic film noir are melancholy, alienation, bleakness, disenchantment, pessimism, ambiguity, moral corruption,

* Originally published as "Blade Runner: An interpretation" in *Psychoanalytic Psychology*, 21(2): 312–318. Copyright © 2004 by the American Psychological Association. Adapted with permission.

evil, guilt, and paranoia. Heroes (or anti-heroes), corrupt characters and villains include down and out hardboiled detectives, or private-eyes, cops, gangsters, government agents, crooks, war veterans, petty criminals and murderers. These protagonists are often morally ambiguous low lifes from the dark and gloomy underworld of violent crime and corruption. Distinctively, they are cynical, tarnished, obsessive (sexual or otherwise), brooding, menacing, sinister, sardonic, disillusioned, frightened and insecure loners (usually men) struggling to survive and ultimately losing.

In brief, these are people on the edge—blade runners! There are other ingredients of *film noir* to which I shall refer later, but the ones I have just mentioned are more than sufficient for a definitive match.

*   *   *

Throughout the voluminous gloss on *Blade Runner*, the theme of the fallen angels has a special place. Writers have identified the Replicants as types for Lucifer and his co-conspirators who, according to Christian legend, were expelled from heaven as a result of their rebellion against God. The story constitutes the subject of Milton's *Paradise Lost* (2001), which explores the relations among creatures along the continuum that Professor Arthur Lovejoy labeled *The Great Chain of Being* (1972), specifically, that part of the chain that links humans with animals at one end, and with angels at the other. Milton is especially interested in humans' relations with the fallen angels who have become devils. For this reason, in chapter three, he recreates the events in the biblical Book of Genesis, in which Adam and Eve succumb to the blandishments of Lucifer to eat of the Tree of Knowledge.

Paradise Lost is the prime example, in English, of a literary epic, a form that is often ranked at the highest level of poetic art. That its themes are imaginatively recast into the mold of a *film noir* demonstrates the devolution of our conception of the heroic as a consequence of the serial disillusionment wrought by historical events involving levels and magnitudes of inhumanity that could no longer be obscured by repression and idealization. Indeed, the film underscores this degradation by the implicit contrast between such *noir* elements as the apocalyptic vision of Los Angeles, the characters of Captain Bryant, Leon, and Zhora, and the cynicism of Holden, on the one hand, and Deckard's dream of the unicorn, on the other. Deckard is, without question, a *noir* antihero, trapped in a net of ontological necessity that renders life nearly unliveable. The unicorn is linked to the white dove that Roy releases shortly before his death. Both signify something pure, spiritual, and elusive, an idealization to which people aspire in an attempt to transcend the increasing meaninglessness, squalor, and sheer Hobbesian viciousness of the entropy that is accelerated by a fatally flawed human nature.

Here, we return to the theme of the fallen angels. Adam and Eve were expelled from the idealized innocence of Eden as a result of their curiosity about the forbidden and, thereby, were relegated to a fallen state. That is, they became flawed creatures because of original sin, and their descendants, all humankind, inherited the flaw. Therefore, anything that flawed humankind, devised or created, no matter how impressive, would be tainted by the inherent imperfection. Thus, as *Blade Runner* clearly demonstrates, the Replicants are literally fatally flawed. Not only is their life span limited to four years, but they have problems in feeling and remembering.

In the confrontation between Leon and Deckard, Leon utters the cryptic, "I tell you nothing is worse than having an itch you can never scratch" (Silverman, n.d.). In context, the line is suggestive but so ambiguous as to be vulnerable to myriad interpretations. This is because it was the last sentence of a far more explicit and elaborated passage in an earlier, discarded draft of the script (Fancher & Peoples, 1980) (see p. 96 above). What the line implies is that the Replicant's tragedy is to be acutely aware of the nature and quality of functions he can never fulfill, which renders him prey to intense and unremitting longing. This makes Roy's petitioning Tyrell for additional years of life more intelligible: he wants time enough to look for, and perhaps find, ways of scratching the primal itches that humans also struggle with, but with at least the possibility of occasional success.

There is something almost satirical in the self-conscious echoing of the Miltonic *agon* in the strained meeting between Roy and Tyrell. The parody results from the fact that the reenactment in *Blade Runner* takes place at a lower level of the "chain of being" to which I referred earlier. God created the angels as his servants. They rebelled against him when he demanded that they worship his son. Man created the Replicants as his slaves. They rebelled against him because they wished to be rid of the limitations that kept them enslaved. The parallel is extended in Roy's asking Tyrell for more life, a yearning that carries associations to the second of the forbidden fruits of Eden.

*   *   *

When considering the Replicant condition (as opposed to the human condition), it is crucial to keep in mind that the Replicants were created to be slaves. An early scene shows an advertising blimp containing garish billboards and vocals urging Americans to relocate to off-world sites to begin life anew with the help of a Replicant slave: "Use your new friend," it blares, "as a personal body servant or a tireless field hand—the custom tailored, genetically engineered humanoid Replicant designed specifically for your needs" (Silverman, n.d.). It would be difficult to miss the deliberate use of descriptors ("field hand;" "body servant") devised by American slave owners to describe attributes of their property. We are, thus, invited to juxtapose the experiences of the Replicant slaves with those of earlier counterparts, most proximally Africans brought to the Americas. These slaves were similar to their masters in possessing human form, human behavior, and human affects; they were different in skin color and physiognomy. The Replicant slaves are similar in form, behavior, and skin color, but presumably different in their affects.

In both cases, the slaves were the recipients of unacceptable and disavowed qualities projected by the non-slaves. Among these qualities are unbridled aggression, polymorphously perverse and prodigious sexuality, scoptophilic curiosity, stupidity, dishonesty, laziness, soullessness, diabolical evil, inhumanity, and unhumanity. Likewise, in both cases, the slave is seen as merely a need gratifier, a part object without needs and privileges of its own. Since the original human sin was motivated by a particular species of curiosity, one that focused on the forbidden, it follows that this trait would be least acceptable and, therefore, most likely to be projected. Freud (1905d) taught that the adult thirst for knowledge, which he called epistemophilia, is a sublimated form of the infantile curiosity about primal and taboo entities, which he called scoptophilia. The initial and primary target of scoptophilia is the parents' genitals and their functions in the primal scene, the act of creation and procreation. It is in this act that we find the confluence of the two principles symbolized by the forbidden fruit of Eden: Knowledge and Life. The object of the child's lust for knowledge is nothing less than the act by which life is created.

Replicants have a unique reason for being obsessed with the act of creation. Humans have the capacity to reproduce themselves; Replicants must be made by humans. Human reproduction requires two sexes and, thus, intercourse; Replicant reproduction is done technologically—they are replicated, not conceived. Human reproduction is the beginning of personal history, memory, and anticipation. Replicant memory is implanted. Returning to Leon's speech about nothing being worse than an itch you cannot scratch, we can now understand that a Replicant's Oedipus complex involves longing for a mother who never was but the false memory of whom can be implanted. If no memory were implanted, however, the longing may be even more painful. Is it any wonder, then, that it is in response to the question about his mother that Leon loses control of his violence and shoots Holden? The Voight-Kampff machine used by blade runners to discriminate humans from Replicants is designed to detect affect from changes in the subject's eye. There is no need for so subtle an instrument to determine Leon's affect.

To speculate, as I have, on the nature of a Replicant's Oedipus complex leads directly to the question of the Replicant superego, for was it not Freud's contention that the superego is heir to the Oedipus complex? We may then be permitted to ask how a creature that has no parents can develop a conscience. If the answer is by the implantation of memory, then the specific memories implanted would have to be such as to give rise to an Oedipus complex. I have already alluded to Leon's sensitivity to questions about his mother. Recall, too, Roy's asking him whether he had retrieved his "precious photos" (Silverman, n.d.). Photographs are important to Rachael's memories, too, lending credence to her reminiscences by providing them with a concrete external correlative. The one she shows to Deckard is of herself with her mother. Mothers, then, would be likely to occupy a central position in all the implanted and external documentation of the invented personal history of a Replicant. Even among humans, unsolicited questions about mothers are likely to provoke a spectrum of reactions from irritation to violence.

Although he does not allude to personal memories or carry photographs of a family he believes to be his own, Roy behaves in a way that clearly reflects his having a conscience. In response to Tyrell's clumsy attempt to console him for his abbreviated life expectancy by telling him he has burned "twice as bright" (Silverman, n.d.; which is another reference to Lucifer whose name, derived from *lux*, Latin for light, means light bearer or light bringer), Roy hangs his head and confesses, "I have done questionable things" (Silverman, n.d.). Clearly, he expects some admonishment from his father/maker, the model—in Freud's theory—for the internalization that lies at the core of the superego. When, instead of the expected (hoped for) reproof, Tyrell replies with the morally bankrupt, "Also extraordinary things. Revel in your time" (Silverman, n.d.), Roy murders him and gouges out his eyes. Because Tyrell, like Oedipus, adopted a willful blindness to his atrocious acts, this is a punishment that fits the crime. Had Tyrell's answer consisted of a moral gesture, Roy would have accepted the reprimand as appropriate justice. Without the behavioral limits engendered by parental morality, the child is left at the mercy of his impulses and is capable of justice only in the crudest, most violent terms.

Early in the film, Tyrell tells Deckard that memories have been implanted in the Replicants to make them easier to control (Silverman, n.d.):

> We began to recognize in them strange obsessions. After all they are emotionally inexperienced with only a few years to store up the experiences which you and I take for granted. If we give them the past, we create a cushion or pillow for their emotions and consequently we can control them better.

In humans, the psychic structure most relevant to the control of primitive affects and actions is the superego. Hence, the past given to the Nexus 6 by Tyrell must conduce to the development of some agency of self-control akin to the human conscience or superego.

* * *

The difference between the projections of white Americans into their black slaves and those of humans into Replicants is that the former involved unconscious fantasy—attributing qualities to others that the others may or may not have had or that could have been induced in them by treating them in particular ways; the latter involved conscious or unconscious engineering in which the disavowed or intolerable characteristics were actually programmed into the recipient.

Hence, the emphasis in *Blade Runner* on eyes. The Replicants have been fitted with remarkable eyes—eyes that can satisfy the scoptophilic curiosity of those who engineered them, by allowing the Replicants to see things that no humans can see: acts of creation, the primal scene on a cosmic scale. When Roy demands, "Morphology, longevity, incept dates," from Chew, the latter answers, "I don't do such stuff. I just do eyes—just genetic design—just eyes," to which Roy responds, "If only you could see what I've seen with your eyes" (Silverman, n.d.). Later, in the climactic scene with Deckard, Roy laments,

> I've seen things you people wouldn't believe. Attack ships on fire off the shoulder of Orion. I watched C-beams glitter in the dark near Tannhauser Gate. All those moments will be lost in time like tears in the rain. Time to die. (Silverman, n.d.)

What these things signify is anyone's guess, but there is about them something colossal, as though Roy had been witness to events akin to the big bang (no pun intended). Of course, eyes are a complex symbol. In addition to curiosity, they may signify the paranoiac sense of being watched, an atmosphere conveyed by the ubiquitous beams of light that seem to penetrate into all of the dark spaces of the intricate sets in an almost random way, at times parodying the effect of klieg lights at a Hollywood premiere, and at others the concentrated flicker of the shaft of light thrown by a film projector. Perhaps these effects are meant to provide a visual correlative for themes of projection and introjection that are central to the film.

*   *   *

Although *Blade Runner* depicts a struggle between humans and Replicants, it is really a work about Eros and death in which protagonists and antagonists are united by their essential flaws, destructiveness, creativity, egocentricity, and heroic grandeur. For this reason, the *film noir* genre is a perfect vehicle for its themes. Unlike *Paradise Lost*, *Blade Runner* in the end treats evil as an omnipresent, implacable force, and although its ultimate source is not clearly specifiable, all creatures are its witting or unwitting agents. Its perspective here is similar to that of Freud. In the film's opening scene, we see Blake's "Dark Satanic Mills" (Milton, 2001, p. 244) reflected in the universal eye, the blasted landscape of a post nuclear Los Angeles, under perpetual rain and smog. We see an abomination, Earth transformed from a green and pleasant Eden to a Hell by human destructiveness, not by villains, but by a tragic destiny that is beyond the power of creatures. We hear the sickeningly familiar commercial blandishments intone, "A new life awaits you in the Off-world colonies, the chance to begin again in a golden land of opportunity and adventure—new climate, recreational facilities . . ." (Silverman, n.d.), and from the very rhetoric of the hundreds of thousands of pandering advertisements to which we have all been exposed, we foresee, with a kind of futile accuracy, how the deadly flaw will be exported to the new sites. Are these not the identical phrases with which Eastern Americans were lured to California? In an ironic reversal, the "Forty acres and a mule" that General Tecumsah Sherman promised to liberated black slaves is here updated as a piece of Off-world land and a Replicant.

This shared tragic destiny is conveyed by the infiltration of vocalized sounds into the music of Vangelis' haunting score. When Roy kills Tyrell, the scream of pain and horror that seems to emerge from the victim is soon indistinguishable from Roy's agonized response; the mask of horror on Tyrell's face is likewise mirrored in Roy's stricken expression. It is difficult to find the demarcations among rage, anguish, and grief on Roy's face during the murder. In the same way, after Roy has begun to pursue Deckard but has paused to grieve over the dead body of Pris, he emits a feral howl that is echoed by Deckard's roar of pain in response to straightening and binding his two broken fingers. Roy seems to experience Deckard's pain, and Deckard experiences Roy's, like instruments in sympathetic vibration but also like antagonists whose frequencies periodically meet in clashing dissonance. Their voices merge with, and emerge from, the encompassing sound track in such a way as to suggest that their suffering is a function of some transcendent force in which they are both trapped. This idea is carried visually by the intricate patterns of light on the dominant dark field.

Each of the opponents has an injured hand. Roy's—with fingernails blackened around the edges in a resemblance to those of the Frankenstein monster—has become necrotic as his time ebbs away. This is a deliberate visual quote to conjure associations to the earlier android, just as the Pinocchio nose of one of Sebastian's toys is meant to remind us of yet another earlier prototype. To prolong his hand's functioning, he pierces the palm with a spike and thereby establishes a similitude with the figure of the crucified Jesus. Simultaneously, Deckard is seen tightening the rag around his two broken fingers, which causes intense pain. While symbolizing their martyrdom to the tragic destiny, the injuries to the hands are also a punishment to the destructive organs that have inflicted so much pain on others. These parallel developments bring the two characters into increasing convergence until, by the end of the scene, they are no longer antagonists but, rather, simultaneous victims and agents of the encompassing struggle between a kind of cosmic entropy and an almost blind groping for an elusive redemption.

Earlier in the scene, Roy hurls his challenge to Deckard, "You'd better get it up or I'm gonna have to kill ya! Unless you're alive, you can't play, and if you can't play . . ." (Silverman, n.d.). The implication is that to be alive is to have to play, and that what it means to play is to see the struggle through to its always fatal end, a struggle that requires its participants both to "Get it up," to maintain an erection, and to get one's arms and weapons up in preparation for an attack— that is, to deploy one's Eros and aggression unconditionally because any other choice is feckless and nihilistic under the rigid rules of the universe. If you do not play, you die anyway, but ingloriously.

Blake (1982), whose influence on the film is considerably greater than Roy's misquotation, put forth the following ideas that could well serve as the motto of this study:

> Without contraries is no progression. Attraction and Repulsion, Reason and Energy, Love and Hate are necessary to human existence. From these contraries spring what the religions call Good and Evil. Good is the passive that obeys Reason. Evil is the active springing from Energy. Good is Heaven Evil is Hell. (p. 123)

These lines emphasize the essential dualism of the universe, its irreducible opposing forces to which both the animate and inanimate must ultimately submit. At the human level, this antithesis gives life its essentially tragic character. Unlike the perspectives of earlier and latter-day neo-Freudians, Freud's view of the universe and of man was consistent with those of Blake, of the creators of *Blade Runner*, and of modern physics. He believed in a creative Eros that is in fundamental, unavoidable conflict with destructiveness and that, in the end, Thanatos is dominant. He also believed in the possibility of generating meaning in the little window that life opens between conception and the void. I am certain that he would also have subscribed to the propositions that each subsequent generation is the beneficiary of the unique meanings forged by their predecessors and that the cumulative record thus formed constitutes culture, a repository of responses to the perennial requirements of living on the edge—of being a blade runner. I believe that, too, and I believe it is what this film is about.

Lord of the Flies: In the beginning was . . . the end

I have chosen to discuss a single aspect of the film's beginning in some depth. This choice is predicated on an accepted principle of all psychotherapy, and in particular of group psychotherapy: to wit, that the start of a session frequently contains the germ of whatever theme is to elaborated later on. In this, the session is comparable to most human projects that have structure and a modicum of duration. In no class of project is this principle more prevalent than in works of art. Accordingly, the overture to an opera or oratorio, the opening scene of a play or novel, the initial theme in a set of variations, are all intended to broach or state the problem that the work will later explore, ramify, or resolve. Perhaps the scene that immediately follows the content-establishing montage of the opening credits is the overture to *Lord of the Flies* (Hook, 1990). If so, closer study of it should contribute to an understanding of the film, as a whole.

The first chapter of the novel on which the film is based is entitled "The sound of the shell." It refers to the use of a conch discovered by Ralph and Piggy as a trumpet to summon the other survivors out of the forest. The conch is, then, in the first instance, a symbol of communication, the principal prerequisite for community. From this relatively crude usage stems the possibility of linguistic evolution towards higher levels of symbolization, conceptual development, and, ultimately, the achievement of culture itself. Implicit in the conch as symbol is the dialectical interdependence and antagonism between the need for society and the need for thought. Each need is fundamental, each requires the other, but each finds in the other a nucleus of intense repulsion. The interface of thought and society is, thus, a locus of continuous struggle that may eventuate in mutual development or mutual destruction. It is also precisely at that interface where group therapists do their most essential work.

Wilfred Bion's formulations with regard to the natural history of small groups (Bion, 1961) provide a useful framework in which to examine the overture to *Lord of the Flies*. His theory of thinking tends, implicitly, to be the mortar that binds his elliptically presented notions of group process into a coherent structure. It follows, then, that whenever Bion uses the term "development," in discussing group activity, he is referring to the possibility of thought and conceptualization. Moreover, he posits that group process is a constant battle between the tendency to defensive stereotypy in the form of basic assumption cultures and the urge to penetrate experience by rational means. The basic assumption cultures—dependency, fight/flight, and pairing—are the group's wonted method of coming to terms with psychotic intensities of anxiety, which, by definition, is primitive and persecutory.

Applying this necessarily sketchy schematization of Bion's ideas to the beginning of the film, we can infer that the major theme involves the vicissitudes of this thin, fragile, yet exquisitely compelling instrument, language, which was called *organon*, literally tool, by Aristotle (2015). Over against the conch stand the basic assumption cultures adumbrated in the sequence of events immediately following Ralph's trumpeting summons. First, there is the demand for a leader or chief, the inevitable yearning for a powerful authority on whom to place one's hopes in the face of the unknown and its attendant terrors. After the selection of the leader, a specialized task group is appointed to administer violence. These are the hunters, formerly the choirboys, whose fight/flight function is thus summarily established. Finally, a signal pairing occurs between Ralph and Jack, already antagonists who, with Simon, their symbolic child between them, set out to explore the island in a peculiar atmosphere of glamor and hopefulness.

Here, then, is the overture. In the scenes that follow, we are to learn of "the Beastie," that sinister presence, seen, yet unseen, within, yet externalized, destroyed, yet immortal, the symbol of pervasive basic anxiety. We shall also be witness to the emergence of a phenomenon that Bion has called a bizarre object, an ego function gone haywire, in the form of the boys' pell-mell rush to build their first disastrous fire. The event also serves to foreshadow the fiery Armageddon with which the film ends. Our attention will be drawn inexorably to the destiny of the conch itself as, in the hands of its faithful steward, Piggy, it is reduced to smithereens which fall with him to the rocky edge of the sea from whence it came.

Between the overture and the final denouement, there is a progressive deterioration of the linguistic function as communication yields to mere expression, and as a society with possibilities for differentiation devolves to the status of an undifferentiated tribe. As a precondition to this process, the two individuals capable of conceptualizing the group's experience are murdered. Simon, the epileptic visionary who interprets the group's projection of its persecutory ideas, is able to be alone, and also to discover the true nature of the apparition on the mountain top, is crucified as he stumbles into the group's atavistic orgy. Piggy, "the soft but persistent voice of reason," is crushed by a boulder which one of Jack's boys has pried loose from its mooring.

The intense hatred for thinking that a group exhibits under the sway of a basic assumption is increasingly in evidence as the film progresses. Gradually, the dialectical balance is irrevocably upset and the implacable pressure for a non-pluralistic organization of clone-like parts overwhelms the groping, tentative quest for mind. One by one, various ego functions are submerged in the agglutinated mass towards which the group tends. Thinking becomes increasingly difficult; perception can no longer distinguish inner from external events; judgment is reduced to reflex; and reality testing falls away like some vestigial organ. In the end, the sound of the shell is silenced, and even its faint echoes are lost amid the Babel-like din that takes the place of coherent language.

Structurally, the overture introduces an antinomy—thought *vs.* basic-assumption activity—that suggests the possibility of an ascending spiral of development. Almost immediately, however, the process assumes a descending course. At intervals throughout the story, equilibrium is re-established at progressively lower levels until, "Things fall apart; the center cannot hold; / Mere anarchy is loosed upon the world, / The blood-dimmed tide is loosed, and everywhere / The ceremony of innocence is drowned" (Yeats, 1983a, pp. 187–188). Each succeeding level juxtaposes the initial antagonists in a less and less equal distribution of power until the dialectic, itself, is fatally compromised. The form and content of the overture are, thus, repeated in the main body of the plot, each repetition punctuated by an "assembly" that recalls and repeats the boys' first convocation in response to the sound of the conch.

All the experiences that are most exciting and most dangerous in group therapy are given dramatic representation in *Lord of the Flies*. The film's virtue (and the novel's) lies precisely in the verisimilitude with which certain concrete situations convey an emotional ambience that is strikingly familiar to anyone who has conducted therapy with groups. For all its flaws, (the self-conscious clutter of symbolism, the protrusive scaffolding of psychodynamics, the cacophonous echoing of the English literary tradition), the novel provides a *mise-en-scène* for those elements of the film that most evoke the phenomenology of basic assumption organization. In this sense, the film, though less rich, is also a less confused, more coherent, and economical vehicle for the book's major themes. Despite its own cinematic flaws, it succeeds in capturing several essential features of group experience in a highly condensed form. As a result, the film, as a whole, belongs to that category of works whose general imperfection is at variance with certain of its discrete components, the rare quality of which rescues it from obscurity.

Seconds: Once more with healing

The problem from which Mr. Hamilton, the Scarsdale banker, suffers is amenable to psychological, psychiatric, or psychoanalytic explanation, but the exclusive use of such an approach would reduce the meaning of *Seconds*. Doubtless, he can be seen as having a depressive disorder, but the diagnosis that seems most appropriate—and this may afford us a clue to some of the wider implications of his situation—is found among the disorders of infancy, childhood, and adolescence. It is called "Identity disorder" (see *DSM IV*, p. 685) and its principal criteria are as follows:

A. Severe subjective distress regarding uncertainty about a variety of issues relating to identity, including three or more of the following:

(1) Long-term goals

(2) Career choice

(3) Friendship patterns

(4) Sexual orientation and behavior

(5) Religious identification

(6) Moral value systems

(7) Group loyalties

Impairment in social or occupational (including academic functioning) as a result of the symptoms in A.

Duration of the disturbance of at least three months.

D. Occurrence not exclusively during the course of a mood disorder or of a psychotic disorder such as schizophrenia.

The disturbance is not sufficiently pervasive or persistent to warrant the diagnosis of a personality disorder.

His problem, then, is that he has never really grown up in the sense that growing up requires an active struggle with life's alternatives, and a passionate commitment to particular ones. What makes this more significant, however, is that generations of American men have been afflicted with a similar disease; indeed, it has been one of the great themes of twentieth-century American literature embodied in such diverse prototypes as Melville's Bartleby (2014), J. Alfred Prufrock (Eliot, 1950a), Marcher, the protagonist of Henry James' *The Beast in the Jungle* (2011), George Babbitt, Sinclair Lewis's Rotarian (1998, 2006), John Updike's Rabbit Angstrom (1960), Hickey, in O'Neill's *The Iceman Cometh* (1957), and Willy Loman (Miller, 1989), the eponymous salesman, all of them in one sense or other, "Hollow-men," to borrow a felicitous phrase from Eliot (1950b).

Hamilton is a particular edition of this prototype, a man of the 1950s, the decade of conformity marked by *I Love Lucy* (1951–1957), Senator Joseph McCarthy, and, in psychoanalysis, Hartmann's (1958) rigid ego psychology with its emphasis on adaptation. Hamilton is a casualty of adaptation, a man who has sickened of his false self, and, because he lacks imagination, nerve, or vision, can think of no way to reach authenticity.

He is, thus, vulnerable to the fantasy of rebirth that has tantalized disaffected Americans time out of mind. It is fundamentally a species of manic reparation requiring, as it does, a destruction of the mnemonic linkage between a past viewed as failed, and an unrealistically idealized future.

*   *   *

Having established a context for the interpretation of *Seconds,* I should like to examine some of the film's details for their unique and disquieting rendition of the theme.

If every opus has an overture that presents the material in condensed form, the overture of *Seconds* is clearly the opening credits in which suffering is conveyed through expressionistic distortions of the flesh reminiscent of Dante, and a Swiftian magnification of the body to the point of disgust and revulsion. The camera bears witness to the transformation by mortification, the essential unnaturalness of the process. It shows us the split between two faces, emphasizing the sensory organs and particularly the mouth that opens in a silent scream, a motif that is repeated when the woman in the set-up rape scene screams silently as Wilson watches the film, when the postsurgical Wilson tries to use his vocal cords prematurely, and when, at last, we actually hear him scream, he is quickly gagged on his way to the operating room.

But there is an interesting contrast in the earlier scene that takes place in Grand Central Station. A man is following Hamilton to slap a slip of paper into his hand with the address of "The Company" written on it. We follow the man for a considerable distance, being shown only the segment from his hat to the bottom of his nose. We never see his mouth. Perhaps the power of autonomous speech is denied those who operate under the aegis of "The Company." Perhaps Hamilton, described by his wife as silent, is unable to find his voice until it is too late. Suddenly, the silent man has too much to say, the taciturn man is overwhelmed with emotion, and the man who was dead wants nothing so much as to live.

Hamilton's conflict about the decision he is making is reflected in the train ride back to Scarsdale. He sweats and looks as though he cannot breathe. The landscape goes by as if for the last time and he seems overwhelmed by the speed that turns the view from the windows into a blur.

The ring of the telephone in his study is sudden and jarring, like an anxiety attack. This effect is repeated in the bank, where an abrupt buzzer marks the opening of a security door and, again, in the day room, to interrupt the cathartic discussion between Wilson and Charlie. Its function is to create anxiety, a sense of urgency regarding the passage of time, and to punctuate endings like a one-way door or valve, an echo, perhaps of the bartender's warning, "Hurry up, please, it's time!" in Eliot's "The Wasteland" (1950c, pp. 402–414).

*   *   *

Hamilton's descent into hell, as Dante's, begins as he steps through an ordinary door and into the tailor shop where silent, sullen men ply their repetitive tasks, and the press is periodically slammed down to produce an obscuring blast of steam. Though he leaves the shop holding the "Company's" new address, he has taken the first irrevocable step into hell. Each subsequent one only takes him deeper.

The segue to the next step is steam—from the hot steam of the pressing machine to the cold steam of the refrigerator plant where beef cadavers prefigure the discussion of human cadavers that will take place in Ruby's office. There is, again, a sense of urgency; the process must go on quickly, incessantly, with no time to lose and no time to think or feel. After Hamilton (now Wilson) is given a white coat, a white-clad side of beef slams brutally into the door, pushing it open. They follow after it, into the cold. The message is obvious: he is being processed like the side of beef, with the same heedless brutality, barely disguised by the thin patina of civility shown by the "Company's" personnel. To emphasize the point, his white coat is inscribed with the words, "Honest Arnie Hi Pro. The Used Cow Dealer." The "Company" is highly professional in its dealing with the dead meat of used animals and humans. As they descend the stairs to the waiting truck, they are seen through silhouettes of heavy chains in the foreground. The chains underscore the sense of harshness, cruelty, and imprisonment, but also symbolize various linkages that are important in the film: the link that the "Company" helps its clients to sever, between their past and future, and the link that Wilson tries to re-forge in his failed struggle.

Among the more devastating images in the film is the depiction of the day room to which Wilson intrudes in his attempt to leave the building after awakening from his drugged sleep. The men in the room convey the kind of desperate, distracted futility that is the feature of all institutions where meaningless waiting is the principal activity. They ignore each other, write in ledgers, watch small television sets or read, like so many lobotomized inmates. The orderly is an all-purpose figure—hospital, nursing home, mental institution—attendant. He looks like a rehabilitated derelict, as do most of the "Company" men. They are not "lost, violent souls, but the hollow men, the stuffed men" (Eliot, 1950b, pp. 414–415).

The scene in Ruby's office constitutes another step in the descent into hell. Suspicious of the food after being drugged, Hamilton declines the offer of dinner, brought—hospital style—on a tray with covered dishes. Ruby's gesture in requesting Hamilton's permission to eat the food, is sadistic, and the menace with which he does so after describing various grisly deaths, courtesy of the "Cadaver procurement section," breaking the chicken bones, and using pronouns in so ambiguous a way as to obscure whether the death is merely an arranged event, or actually Hamilton's, deepens the theme introduced by the sides of beef in the meat packing plant. The death to which he alludes is Hamilton's spiritual death, as well as the literal one that will occur when he is "requisitioned from the day room stock on May 6th," having been "released for cadaver use last night." This cruelty parallels Ruby's earlier sardonic agreement with Hamilton's protest that he is not a client yet.

At this point in the film, we are introduced to one of its most brilliant creations, the old man—founder and director of the "Company"—seated, unseen, behind Hamilton dressed in the quintessentially American garb, and with the manner of a cross-denominational clergyman/snake oil salesman/pastoral counselor/avuncular figure/psychotherapist. The pattern of his speech and silence provokes some remarkable reflections and confessions from Hamilton. Describing his marriage, he says, "We get along. What does it all mean?" He acknowledges that he never thought about it before. Then he adds, "We hardly ever quarrel; not that that's any measure of our lives." The old man responds, "This is what happens to the dreams of youth," and later, "There never was a struggle in the soul of a good man that wasn't hard. My Papa told me that. Believe me, Son, I know." Deeply moved, Hamilton murmurs, "I believe you." We are now aware that the old man is the equivalent to Hamilton of the devil in the early morality plays, in *Faust* (Goethe, 1993), and in *Pilgrim's Progress* (Bunyan, 2004). His seductive, quasi-parental, cajoling, soothing words and manner coax Hamilton to relinquish his final resistance to becoming a client, as he signs the contract with the "Company."

The character of the old man condenses two functions that represent profound currents in American culture: salesmanship and religion. This wholly original version of Satan draws upon the unique American development that allowed for the merger of God and Mammon, the mass marketing of religious precepts by a clergy that has embraced Madison Avenue, and the imbuing of salesmen with evangelical zeal, persuading them, that is, to believe so passionately in the product that they cannot help but persuade others to believe in it. This merger has contributed as much as any other social force to the triumph of the U.S. economy: when you can gain mass acceptance for the idea that God and profit are, if not identical, at least mutually potentiating, you have devised a formula for infinite growth by geometric increments. But you have, by the same stratagem, corrupted the spiritual foundation of an entire people and laid the groundwork for the proliferation of a character structure that lacks wholeness, purpose, and integrity, an individual who longs for a utopian future as an antidote to a meaningless present—in short, an Arthur Hamilton.

* * *

Listen to his alter ego, Antiochus Wilson's conversation with Charlie in the day room at the "Company" headquarters after he has returned for reprocessing. He says, "You sounded like this whole thing was something tremendous, the rebirth, everything, even though you haven't made a go of it." Charlie replies, "I thought you'd have a better chance." Wilson says,

> I couldn't help it, Charlie, I had to find out where I went wrong. The years I've spent trying to get all the things I was told were important, that I was supposed to want—things, not people or meaning, just things. It's going to be different from now on, a new face, a new name. I'll do the rest! I know it's going to be different.

The loud buzzer interrupts their talk but Charlie is weeping like a man who has just received enlightenment, and Wilson, for the first time, shows an untroubled smile.

The scene just described might have been derived in language and theme from *Death of a Salesman*. What knits them together is the psychological devastation wrought by false values.

There is an earlier moment, just after Wilson's surgery, when he is brought to the office of his advisor who, ironically, is played by the same actor (Khigh Dhiegh) who played the brainwasher in *The Manchurian Candidate* (1962), an earlier Frankenheimer film. He says to Wilson,

> You are accepted. You are alone in the world, absolved of all responsibility except to your own interest. Isn't that marvelous? You've got

what almost every middle aged man in America would like to have: freedom! Real freedom.

His proposed ideal is a narcissistic personality disorder, and when, later, Wilson has to live this experience, he reacts only with nausea, or Sartre's (1938) *La nausee.*

Such a conception of freedom and the good life derives ultimately from a notion of progress that is inherent in a major strain of American culture. It is that trend that has given impetus to such phenomena as "born again," "*Baal Tshuvah,*" such indigenous American therapies and quasi-therapies as EST, the human-potential movement, the power of positive thinking, twelve-step programs, sales promotion, faith healing, conversion-like experiences, the various notorious apocalyptic cults, evangelism, utopianism, and the general belief in perfectibility. Along with plastic surgery, compulsive fitness, and the morbid fear of aging, these entities seem to flourish in California, the terminus of the American frontier, and the end of the American dream. In his last confession to the old man (note the confessional-like screen in the room), Wilson says, "I guess I never had a dream. If I did have one, it certainly wasn't Antiochus Wilson."

This *zeitgeist* maintains that evil inheres not in human beings, but in corrupt human institutions; when the institutions are changed or rooted out, people will be perfectible. Schemes for human improvement that arise from it regard the child as a *tabula rasa* whom society has tainted. Their goal is to restore the innocence of childhood and their technique involves a species of exorcism or an extended purification ritual. The product of this process is one who has been born-again, reborn, purified, basically divested of the tainted qualities acquired from the corrupt society and, hence, free to pursue perfection.

Among psychoanalytic theories, this position is represented by the so-called neo-Freudian culturalists, the Sullivanians, the Horney-eyans, the Reichians and neo-Reichians, and, yes, the Hartmannian ego psychologists. I deliberately use the term "so-called neo-Freudians," because, as Kovel (1989) and others have pointed out, there are no neo-Freudians, only neo-Adlerians. Freud, unlike Adler, never accepted the notion of an innate human innocence. He viewed aggression, sadism, destructiveness, etc., as inherent in the human endowment, co-eternal with sexuality and affection. For Freud, therefore, therapy involved not the excising of the evils of the past, but an affective familiarization with their derivatives, to attain a degree of control over them. Thus, Freud's view is fundamentally historical and integrative. It stresses the continuity and wholeness of personality. The neo-Freudians foster a discontinuity in which the undesirable past is severed from the perfect future.

* * *

Antiochus Wilson is a failed utopian. Given the opportunity to eschew his past, he finds that he cannot, without obliterating his own sense of continuity and identity, and without the chance of repairing his past failures in their own context. Thus, he becomes alienated from the alienated. Unable to embrace a solution that requires the obliteration of history, he experiences a crisis of identity. His second chance is really the deprivation of a second chance. Had he remained in the life he had been living, he would have had an opportunity to alter it for the better, but he chose to abandon it for a kind of hell, a place of the undead. In this light, the "Company" is a punitive moral agency.

Among the film's most poignant and revealing scenes is the one that takes place in Wilson's bedroom at the "Company." It opens with a view of the confessional screen lighted from behind and, with a sudden flare of the bedside lamp, Wilson is awakened from sleep, the old man seated on the edge of the bed, peering at him with a tricky benevolence. As always, he carries a book, as though he were a clergyman.

I shall quote liberally from this scene because I think it ties together many of the thematic loose ends. Wilson believes he is going to be given a third chance and a new identity. He says, "This time, I've got to be allowed, sir, to make my own decisions." The old man nods, and, a few lines later, says,

> You see, I got tremendous comfort that in my small way, I was waging a battle against human misery, and I was, too, except we do have a high percentage of failures. I guess that's to be expected. But it hurts me. Some reborns make a go of it. We're always working to find ways to improve the system. Yeah, we make mistakes. Fact is, when I saw our clients coming back here, I wanted to chuck the whole thing. But I couldn't. The organization was pretty big by then: a board of directors on a profit sharing basis. All those people. You have no idea what

a financial responsibility it turned into. Tsk, tsk. We make mistakes, but we admit 'em and go forward. I won't see it in my lifetime, but some of the younger execs, like Ruby, may. Oh, you can call it wishful thinking, son, but life is built on wishes and you just gotta keep plugging away at 'em. You can't give up, and you can't let the mistakes jeopardize the dream.

At this point, the gurney arrives to take Wilson to the OR. Wilson speaks urgently: "I've got to talk to you. I didn't expect . . . so soon." The old man replies, "Efficiency! You're lucky we got a match so soon."

Wilson: There's things we have to talk about—my identity and all.

Old Man: We will, we will, later.

Wilson: The thing about doing it on my own. It is so important— choice! We gotta change! We have to talk about it.

Old Man: We will. I'll look into it personally. Just remember, son, we've got to keep plugging away at the dream. The mistakes teach us how. It wasn't wasted.

The scene conveys the workings of the repetition compulsion in the creation of false hope for both participants. Believing he has not been given a choice, Wilson yearns for yet another chance. He fails to understand that it was he who renounced choice when he sold his soul to the "Company." In consequence, no matter how many rebirths he is given, he is destined to fail.

Likewise, the old man cannot renounce his dream despite its repeated failures. He ascribes this, in part, to the growth of the "Company" and its attaining an autonomous power that cannot be resisted, but it is also clear that the dream is of tremendous personal significance to him. Here is a critique of the corporate ethos. The company originates as an attempt to fulfill its founder's dream. It gains a momentum of its own. The failure of many of its products leads the founder to feel disillusioned but he has lost the power to dissolve the "Company." By cognitive dissonance, he must remain and redouble his belief in the dream.

If the old man is a Mephistopheles to Wilson's Faust, he is a peculiarly modern version: a fallen angel divested of the tragic grandeur of a Lucifer because he has no defiant will. He is nothing more than an instrument of the punitive moral agency that the "Company" symbolizes. As self-deluded as his clients, he carries out cosmic justice without knowing it. If Wilson is destined to repeat his error, so is Satan. The film affords us a glimpse into *The Castle* (Kafka, 1992), *The Penal Colony* (Kafka, 1963), and the White Whale (Hayford & Parker, 1967). It shows us that these are merely engines of retribution made possible by false beliefs, by the need to pretend that viciousness, ugliness, destructiveness, decay, dissolution, ennui, boredom, decadence, and all of the other qualities that comprise the idea of evil, can be left behind when we turn our faces towards the light.

We learn, however, that Wilson did have a dream after all. He dreams it just before dying. It is an image of an adult male carrying a child on his shoulders and walking on a beach. It is not clear whether he is the child or the father, but it hints at the necessity for generational support as the primary condition for emotional growth.

CHAPTER FIVE

Conclusion: critical flicker fusion

I have appropriated the title of my book from psychophysics, where it is defined in various complex ways but is essentially the frequency at which a light must flash to be seen by an observer as continuous. It is the principle behind cinema, which is nothing more than the serial presentation of many still pictures at a speed sufficient to make them appear to be a moving image. Taken separately, however, the words serve to underscore my authorial intentions. I do, indeed, assume the role of critic in each of the essays about a particular film. My rendition of the role is weighted heavily towards appreciation. That is, I like and admire the films I have written about and only rarely call attention to defects or flaws in them. In fact, I freely acknowledge that my enthusiasm for almost all these films tends to diminish any capacity or inclination I might have to see their weaknesses. Doubtless, I am much biased to conceive the task of criticism as the enhancement of understanding, appreciation, and pleasure.

The word *flicker* calls attention to a fundamental quality of films, their presentation in a darkened theater where the variability of light and shadow contributes to an atmosphere of fascination, magic, and mystery, not unlike the prevailing ambience of dreams. I think that consciousness is so altered in such a setting that inner and outer reality are less clearly demarcated, creating possibilities for interpenetration that yield new and unforeseen experiences.

Fusion refers, in part, to these unique experiences, but also, I hope, to the way my critical instrument interacts with the flickering images and finds resonance in the eyes and minds of my readers. Further, it carries my aspiration to rescue the disparate elements of the films and of my remarks about them from the matrices of language of which they are necessarily made, to attain a novel coherence.

Introduction

The three appendices are relevant to the similarities among films, dreams, and clinical psychoanalysis. The reader may find these comparisons and contrasts useful in thinking about the films I have discussed and my psychoanalytic approach to them.

Mise-en-scène: session, film, dream

Explication of texts has been conducted by diverse cultures and professions for thousands of years, as has the explication of images. The explication of moving images, though more recent, was prefigured in the interpretation of dreams, an ancient practice, and later, of theater. Psychoanalysts have applied the skills and knowledge necessary to discover meaning in verbal, postural, gestural, narrative, and pictorial human behavior, to the study of films. Among the earliest but still most frequent of such applications are attempts to analyze characters in films as though they were people or patients. Another use of psychoanalytic principles has been in attempts to elucidate the personality of the director or auteur of a particular film or oeuvre.

My intention in this section will be to discover convergent and discriminant elements in the processes of experiencing, understanding, and using psychoanalytic sessions, the dreams that may be a feature of them, and films. The term *mise-en-scène* in my title is a way of describing the unique synthesis of visual, verbal, auditory, and kinetic elements that must be taken into account by any exploration of meaning.

Throughout my discussion, I try to compare works of human creativity with the lived experience from which they are made, to underscore the centrality of reflection and contemplation to mental and emotional complexity. I also talk about perceptual and attentional processes, in relation to the distribution of cathexes. Where useful, I illustrate aspects of my discourse with examples from films about which I have written.

Of the psychoanalytic session depicted in a film, we can say, paraphrasing Magritte (1929), *Ceci n'est pas une psychoanalytique session*. (I am here referring Magritte's 1929 painting of a pipe, with the caption *"Ceci n'est pas une pipe"* printed beneath. The title of the painting is *The Treachery of Images*.) The elements of such a depiction are derived from a prototype of possible psychoanalytic sessions for their dramatic potential, and then shaped and adapted to the purposes of the film by means of film techniques. Similarly, one can say of the material chosen by a psychoanalyst to be included in a paper or presentation, *Ceci n'est pas une psychoanalytique session*, because the analyst, like the filmmaker, selects it from among many clinical specimens for its potential interest to, and influence on, his colleagues. Likewise, the account of a psychoanalytic session presented to a supervisor by a candidate is not a psychoanalytic session but a representation of one, edited to affect the supervisor in certain ways.

The question, then, is "What is a psychoanalytic session if these are not one?" How does a psychoanalytic session differ from these depictions? Why, and to what degree, are they different? The session, like Magritte's picture of a pipe, is contained in a frame. In this particular, it is more like the picture than the pipe. Unlike the frame of the session, however, Magritte's frame lacks two dimensions, those of time and depth. But since the framed session contains sounds, sights, and movement, it is more like a film than a painting or still photograph. So, the similarity between a session and a film has to do with the frame and the perceptual stimuli. Among the differences are that most films are scripted and designed, whereas sessions are extemporaneous, the environment held constant. Films are made to entertain or instruct, whereas the manifest purpose of sessions is to ameliorate suffering and perplexity. Most films show a number of people in a variety of actions; sessions ordinarily consist of two people talking about a variety of actions involving other people.

The goal of the film-maker is to create significance, the characteristic of every perception that carries the promise of meaning. That is, there is a property of the thing perceived that, like ore to a prospector, signals the presence of something valuable. The film-maker creates significance by selecting and arranging elements to compel extraordinary concentrations of attention from audiences. In a film theater, the attention ordinarily distributed among self, others, and surround is focused on the screen, on the visual and auditory imagery. This is similar to the topographic regression that Freud said is essential to dreaming, and it has a kindred effect—an altered state of consciousness that conduces to what Coleridge (1967, p. 452) termed "A willing suspension of disbelief." The mind, in this state, becomes receptive to an expanded range of impressions and ideas, a susceptibility that is exploited by the film-maker, who uses every device in his repertoire in the attempt to attain levels of intensity powerful enough to breach the audience's threshold of significance.

Coleridge's (and Wordsworth's) intentions in publishing the *Lyrical Ballads* are admirably congruent with those of any contemporary artist. He wrote:

> It was agreed, that my endeavours should be directed to persons and characters supernatural, or at least romantic, yet so as to transfer from our inward nature a human interest and a semblance of truth sufficient to procure for these shadows of imagination that willing suspension of disbelief for the moment, which constitutes poetic faith. Mr. Wordsworth on the other hand was to propose to himself as his object, to give the charm of novelty to things of every day, and to excite a feeling analogous to the supernatural, by awakening the mind's attention from the lethargy of custom, and directing it to the loveliness and the wonders of the world before us . . . (Coleridge, 1967, p. 452)

Coleridge's phrase "shadows of the imagination" is a remarkably apt designation both for the material and atmosphere of dreams and a "willing suspension of disbelief" typifies the attitude of dreamers. Like films, dreams are fictions. They are interesting to the dreamer because they are his, but, more relevantly, because they are hallucinatory, cryptic, disquieting, or perhaps disturbing, and not least because they are steeped in a medium so divergent from waking experience as to appear surreal. Again, borrowing from Magritte, the report of a dream that a patient brings to a session *"N'est pas un rêve."* We are all too familiar with the transformations affected upon the original dream prior to its being shared with others to believe that its narration is any more veridical than those of so called eye-witness accounts of events or of anyone's recollections of his own past.

Dreams, like quotidian waking experience, are unframed, but resemble films in the way they hijack attention and perception while restricting motor activity. Psychoanalytic sessions, as many have observed, derive many of their features from the conditions of dreaming: the supine position, the relative immobility, and the milder, yet prevalent sensory deprivation that tends to direct attention to mentation. If films are made to entertain, and sessions to help, what is the purpose of dreams? Despite our Freudian bias, and the myriad theories of dreams advanced from ancient times until now, it is generally agreed only that people are fascinated by them and insatiably curious about their meaning. Their metaphorical structure, the compression and vividness of their imagery, and the elusiveness of their purport rivet the attention of the dreamer and often those to whom the dream is told. Perhaps their action in "... awakening the mind's attention from the lethargy of custom," is essential to human existence in some, as yet incompletely explained, way. It is as though the effort necessary to accommodate "the great blooming, buzzing confusion" (James, 1890, p. 462) that is waking life calls for an antithesis, a world that requires no adaptation, only acceptance.

So far, I have said little about everyday waking experience, the ground of most people's lives, against which films, sessions, and dreams stand forth. To be sure, there are transcendent moments in our waking lives that are as distinct from the ordinary as the entities we have been examining, but they are, almost by definition, exceptional. They take place in a form of time that was called *kairos* by the ancient Greeks, a moment of the momentous. In contrast, the continuity of ordinary occurrence was given the name "*chronos*." I think it is the hope of all film-makers, analysands, analysts, and dreamers to create the conditions of *kairos*. The question this leads to is whether and how this happens in the psychoanalytic session.

If, as I have already said, film-makers use every technique at their disposal to rivet the attention of their audiences in the hope of conveying significance, does something similar happen in the analytic session and is it desirable? Psychoanalytic sessions, like films and dreams, partake of fiction. They differ from films and dreams in that they are not likely to be inherently interesting. Indeed, one of the reasons for their existence is that the stories told by their protagonists have been serially rejected by audiences to whom they have been previously told and performed. As a result, their authors have sought recourse to an audience, the analyst, whose expertise includes the ability to pay attention to performances that have failed in earlier iterations.

Here, let us recall my point that simulacrums depicted in films, and described in analytic papers and by candidates in supervision, are not psychoanalytic sessions. The reason is that most psychoanalytic sessions tend to be deficient in the eidetic, radiant, or otherwise exciting qualities sought after by film-makers, dreamers, supervisees, and other people seeking something akin to what Maslow (1964, p. 5) called "Peak experiences."

Most sessions consist of reports from the analysand of ordinary life events as well as more-or-less failed attempts to follow the fundamental rule. Anyone who has watched episodes of *In Treatment* (Garcia et al., 2008–2011), or meetings between Tony Soprano and Dr. Melfi would attest that they are not representative of the domain. How, then, is it possible for analyst and analysand to give this material the requisite attention?

I have shown elsewhere (Fried, 2010) that one of the effects of transference is that it allows the analyst to entertain the fiction that any of the patient's references to the people and events in his life may be communications about him, in disguised form. Put another way, transference is, among other things, a conceit, in both senses of the term, that engages the analyst's attention because its substance is assumed to be pointedly personal. Conversely, if the analysand is receptive to the implications of transference interpretations, he comes to believe that any of his verbalizations may be addressed to the figure from his own inner life whom he has projected to the analyst. These reciprocal assumptions result, potentially, in the creation of a highly charged atmosphere that is akin in vividness, excitement, and significance to that of a film or a dream. Transference may thus be regarded as the equivalent of the analyst's membership in the union of actors who are assigned roles in the patient's film or drama.

The coda to these reflections is that we must be cautious in our understanding and use of all the devices exploited by artists, analysts, and dreamers, to heighten the perception of, and receptiveness to, experience. We must remember that they are fictions, not myths. To elucidate this, I have recourse to the words of the critic, Frank Kermode (1966, p. 39):

We have to distinguish between myths and fictions. Fictions can degenerate into myths whenever they are not consciously held to be fictive . . . Myth operates within the diagrams of ritual, which presupposes total and adequate explanation of things as they are and were; it is a sequence of radically unchangeable gestures. Fictions are for finding things out, and they change as the needs of sense-making change. Myths are the agents of stability, fictions the agents of change. Myths call for absolute, fictions for conditional assent. Myths make sense in terms of a lost order of time, *illud tempus* as Eliade calls it; fictions, if successful, make sense of the here and now, *hoc tempus.*

So let us open our minds to the stories we invent and invest with the semblance of reality so that we can use them to change, yet always retain the prerogative of redeploying our disbelief.

Whatever flames upon the night

All representation derives ultimately from the hallucination by which the infant tries to restore the primordial experience of oneness or merger that preceded the first separation. All subsequent representation bears the indelible stamp of this prototype, either quite visibly or under camouflage. The hallucination is a memory trace raised to the status of a percept. When it fails, as it must, to restore this original or ur-state, its eidetic qualities recede; it becomes only a memory. But it also becomes the prototype for all further representation as well as the seed of the phenomenon we call transference.

The principal goal of representation is to preserve pleasurable experiences, as when people take snapshots of vacations, parties, births, etc. Technology has enabled an impressive expansion of the methods for preservation. This can be described along a continuum that would begin with the memory trace, and proceed sequentially through drawing, painting, sculpture, writing, photography, and moving pictures, to virtual reality devices. The continuum shows a trend towards ever more accurate and detailed reproduction because its aim is nothing less than the reinstatement of the original. Witness the movement to increasingly punctilious verisimilitude in film-making that hijacks all the frame's visual space, leaving little room for the creative perception of the viewer.

All this is at the service of controlling time, rescuing moments of gratification from its flux, and letting the rest—variants of pain or boredom—slip by. We hope, eventually, to tip the scales as much towards gratification as possible, to give permanence to something ephemeral. By these strategies we gain partial respite from the agony of separateness along with a preview of the longed-for coming attraction, the return to paradise and abrogation of time. Also, along the way, if we are able, we may discover that renunciation of the ur-goal may engender an entirely different order of representation, valuable in itself. Of this, more later.

Now, the enterprise of representation has always been problematic and dangerous. Recall the second of the Ten Commandments (Genesis, 1973–77): "Thou shalt not make unto thee any graven image or any likeness of any thing that is in heaven above or that is in the earth beneath, or that is in the water under the earth."

God specifically enjoins visual representation of any sort on pain of severe punishment. To judge from the additional language and import of the book of Genesis, this making of images seems, like the knowledge of good and evil, and the forbidden tree of life, to be the jealous preserve of God. Likewise, the authoring of texts and narratives, epitomized by scripture itself, was God's exclusive province; man, exemplified by Moses, was a mere scribe or amanuensis. By tradition, neither the poet nor prophet originated their words but were only vessels through which the divine might speak.

Two other instances in which divine prerogatives were stolen are most relevant to our discourse. Prometheus paid dearly for stealing fire from the gods, and Lucifer was expelled from heaven for challenging God's authority. Both embody the quality of light: fire implies enlightenment and technology; Lucifer is Latin for "bringer of light." Light is what films are made of, and light is both the tool and goal of analysis.

If it was considered a sin to create images, narratives, technology, and analysis, was it because all these constituted ways of pursuing the wish to recreate paradise, utopia, the golden age, nirvana, or, most simply, quiescence? Was the longing for these states considered so subversive and destructive as to be anathematized or did the danger inhere in the possibility that people might discover divergent alternatives? Did constituted authority consider it necessary to appropriate to itself the distribution of rewards for obedience and place them exclusively at the end of life? There is a deeply problematic relationship between the naïve belief in progressively greater accuracy of representation, on the one hand, and capturing the obscure object of desire, on the other.

So, film-makers came gradually to understand that they, too, could market a visual vehicle for narrative that emulated the traditional pattern in which stability is undermined by crisis, antagonistic forces contend for dominance, the good prevail, the bad are punished, and order is restored. This model both confirmed and reinforced public expectations. Despite the peripeteia or swerve in circumstances, the status quo could be restored and people could live happily ever after. Using this format, they developed a method to translate the verbal and pictorial conventions of stage plays into the more fluid and fundamentally visual medium of cinema. Audiences derived intense satisfaction from the inherent knowledge that, no matter the degree of sound and fury, the film, unlike their lives, would end at a precisely predictable moment with all contradictions resolved. It was only a matter of time.

If the aphorism attributed to Kafka, "The meaning of life is that it ends," is valid in any sense, then films that end with the protagonists' living happily ever after have no meaning. To attain meaning, a film, like any other work of the imagination, must address the immanence of death. This requires a definitive renunciation of the possibility of a return to any original state of merger, as symbolized by the Eden myth, and a concomitant acceptance of the struggle with life's vicissitudes. Such a renunciation results in a very different kind of film, one devoid of certainty and reassurance but offering up an occasion for contradiction and reflection.

A cultural development that provided the impetus and inspiration for this new conception of narrative was the publication of James Joyce's Ulysses (2009) in defense of which Ezra Pound (1921) wrote, "Life for the most part does not happen in neat little diagrams and nothing is more tiresome than the continual pretence that it does." Those who cannot renounce the ur experience will be given to repetitive temporizing to await the beatific moment. They will be unable to die because they will not have lived.

Patients often enter analysis or therapy with the implicit fantasy of finding, possessing, and being possessed by the obscure object of desire. In the early days of psychoanalysis, this fantasy had its counterpart in the analysts' assumption that if the circumstances of the patient's infancy and childhood could be "reconstructed," s/he would be cured. I think they imagined this reconstruction as an affective re-living of the original situation, accurate in every particular. What patients, but more especially analysts, had eventually to give up, was that such a reconstruction was possible. The source of most resistance in psychoanalysis is a failure to make this renunciation on both sides of the couch. It is also implicated when analyses become interminable or prematurely ended. In the event the renunciation is successful, however, the dyad will be freed to create a viable narrative in which the ending is by no means known or assured.

If we steal the prerogatives of God or the gods with the sole intention of delaying the moment of death indefinitely, we are damned. If we steal fire, light, understanding, and story telling to explore the region eastward of Eden, we should be able to stop worrying about redemption.

> Wild men who caught and sang the sun in flight
> And learn, too late, they grieved it on its way,
> Do not go gentle into that good night.
> (Thomas, 1971, p. 128)

Thus, all representation is about time and death. We want to catch the sun in flight: what could be a more apt description of filmmaking? Catching the sun in flight is a metaphor for the control of light that is the essence of moving pictures. But we learn that our attempts at preserving do not succeed in arresting time, only in delaying and beguiling it as we wait to go ungently into that good night, uncertain of how or when we shall die.

Winnicott's rich legacy includes nothing of greater utility and significance than the set of ideas he developed under the rubric, "transitional object." Here is a succinct summary of the concept:

> The transitional objects and transitional phenomena belong to the realm of illusion which is at the basis of initiation of experience. This early stage in development is made possible by the mother's special capacity for making adaptation to the needs of her infant, thus allowing the infant the illusion that what the infant creates really exists.

This intermediate area of experience, unchallenged in respect of its belonging to inner or external (shared) reality, constitutes the greater part of the infant's experience and throughout life is retained in the intense experiencing that belongs to the arts and to religion and to imaginative living, and to creative scientific work.

A positive value of illusion can therefore be stated.

An infant's transitional object ordinarily becomes gradually decathected, especially as cultural interests develop. (Winnicott, 1953, p. 97)

Donald Winnicott explained that the child does not mourn the discarded transitional object because he redistributes his interest from it to the entire domain of culture, an entity made of time–space and secondary objects. Films, like novels, plays, certain poems, and other narratives belong to culture.

Borrowing from the ancient Greeks, I should like to describe a framework for thinking about our several approaches to time. They used the word *kairos* to denote a special, qualitative moment in which significant events occur. It is not really time at all, but a suspension of it, the equivalent of holding one's breath in anticipation of something extraordinary. In contrast, they reserved the word *chronos* for the ordinary, quotidian passage of time. *Chronos* is sequential; *kairos* is singular and unique.

We can conceive of two versions of *kairos*, the first involving such sought after magical interludes as those that James Joyce (1944) called epiphanies, Virginia Woolf (1985) named "moments of being," and the Russian film director, Andrei Tarkovsky recently termed the "sculpting of time." *Kairos* takes another, more extreme, form in such experiences as merger, nirvana, and death, described by mystics and visionaries. Whereas time is suspended in the former, in the latter, time is extinguished.

Chronos, too, manifests in a number of ways, for example as anxiety, depression, and boredom, a triad that may be labeled persecutory. A second triad of *chronos* consists of action, power, and value. These are associated with fantasies of controlling or conquering time. Persecutory *chronos* frequently instigates addictive behavior such as drug use, excessive recourse to electronic media, food, sex, exercise, etc. The expedients intended to control or conquer time may include unremitting activity, and the construction of monuments such as statues, buildings, works of art, progeny, and systems of thought. At their most extreme, they inspire the development of eschatology.

One enterprise that partakes of all these strategies is the creation of fiction, by which I mean writing, film, painting, music, and clinical psychoanalysis. Thus, the transitional object to which Winnicott directed our attention is replaced by culture in these forms. The ones that concern us in this book are films, psychoanalysis, and everyday life. My thesis is that cinematic and analytic stories, and those improvised to suit the occasions of our daily routines, deal with the challenge of time in some combination of the strategies I have described.

For example, I believe I am justified in suggesting that we use fiction to achieve the aim of prolonging and extending time, while forestalling death or its intermediate representative, endings. We do this by means of a species of narrative that we may call the Scheherezade effect, after the Persian legend in which a young woman learns of a king whose dissatisfaction with a succession of prospective wives has led him to kill each one in turn. She asks to be considered for the job, and uses the technique of telling the king a story every night, one that is interrupted by a cliffhanger. When asked about the ending, she says there is not sufficient time that night; consequently, the story will have to be continued on the next night. In this way, she succeeds in remaining alive for a thousand and one nights, at the end of which the king marries her. This legend is a useful symbol of our own ways of struggling with the tyranny of time. It will surprise no one that the legend resembles, in every essential, what we all did as children when we asked our parents to tell us a story at bedtime to postpone the moment of separation, when we were forced to surrender to sleep and relax our vigilant scrutiny of the link between mother and father.

One of the reasons we make fictions is to overcome helplessness: we identify with the aggressor, presumably God, the creator, who has made the comprehensive fiction in which we exist and to which we must respond. Put in another way, we create our own fictions in order not to be imprisoned in someone else's. We also attempt to harness time by changing its velocity, speeding it up or slowing it down. Nowhere is this more apparent than in films. It can occur in real time, as does the classic American Western, *High Noon* (Kramer, 1952), where the tempo-as-we-live-it lends every event, down to the merest gesture, the significance of a *chronos* heightened by escalating degrees of action, the oscillation of power, and a constant juxtaposition of goodness *vs.* evil. It can be slowed by an epiphany, such as the scene in John Huston's film, *The Dead* (1987), in which Gabriel sees his wife Gretta transfixed on the staircase as she listens to a song sung to her years before by a boy she had loved. Joyce's definition of epiphany corresponds in salient particulars to the concept of *kairos*.

> By an epiphany, he meant "a sudden spiritual manifestation", whether in the vulgarity of speech or of gesture or in a memorable phase of the mind itself. He believed that it was for the man of letters to record these epiphanies with extreme care, seeing that they themselves are the most delicate and evanescent of moments. He told Cranly that the clock of the Ballast Office was capable of an epiphany. Cranly questioned the inscrutable dial of the Ballast Office with his no less inscrutable countenance:
>
> –Yes, said Stephen. I will pass it time *after* time, allude to it, refer to it, catch a glimpse of it. It is only an item in the catalogue of Dublin's street furniture. Then all at once I see it and I know at once what it is: epiphany.
>
> –What?
>
> –Imagine my glimpses at that clock as the gropings of a spiritual eye which seeks to adjust its vision to an exact focus. The moment the focus is reached the object is epiphanised. It is just in this epiphany that I find the third, the supreme quality of beauty. (Joyce, 1944)

I do not think it accidental that Joyce chose a clock to illustrate his idea. The moment when *chronos* transitions to *kairos* is most directly represented by a clock that has stopped.

Just as film-makers create narratives for audiences, the analysand collaborates with her analyst to create a narrative that differs from the one she was given early in her life. That narrative has been spoken and enacted in myriad ways. She is the protagonist of her own play. One of the motives for her seeking psychotherapy is that she has been play-acting, that is, enacting a role in her play. Among the goals she is seeking are to stop play-acting and enacting, and to start playing and acting. To act, in this context, means to depart from the received script, to improvise, to do things differently. To play means to live, for as long as may be necessary, in imaginative circumstances where variability of all kinds is possible. It entails the willing suspension of disbelief and what Marianne Moore (1970, pp. 370–371), described as "imaginary gardens with real toads in them," in a wonderful metaphor of transference.

Back in the day when healing was considered a comprehensive human endeavor, Hippocrates (1996–2016), admonished doctors that, "Art is long, life is short, opportunity fleeting, experiment treacherous, and judgment difficult." It seems fitting then that we have used some time in this short life as a fleeting opportunity to contemplate duration in art by advancing risky ideas and attempting difficult judgments.

Mad doctors

"There are some things, Professor, that man was not meant to know."
Variations on this line are spoken in almost every film in which the
explorations of a "mad" doctor, scientist, etc. transgress the imaginary
border between the realms of legitimate inquiry and domains considered taboo or forbidden. An older colleague, who represents the views
of respectable science, usually speaks the line. His judgment is a state-
ment of the norms and standards of society in the field of science and,
as such, is a product of the civilized conscience or superego. It stands
as a warning to the few investigators in any age whose imagination
and audacity take them beyond what is considered to be true and
accepted. The idea is one of the oldest and most tantalizing in the
Western tradition, beginning with the account of Eve's temptation in
the Book of Genesis. According to the Biblical story, Eve is tempted by
the serpent (Devil) to eat of the forbidden fruit of the tree of knowledge, thus acquiring access to the criteria for distinguishing good
from evil. From this auspicious beginning, the theme of diabolic temptation radiates through the folklore, legends, and literature of the
world.

Unable to own the responsibility and consequences of his own
curiosity, man ascribes his actions in quest of the unknown to an evil

force. But, because even this chain of cause and effect is too short for comfort, he adds to it another link, in the form of woman, the creature who—by means of projection—becomes the locus of his moral weakness. So now, it is the Devil (the evil one) who tempts the woman (the weak one) to explore forbidden realms, and the man (the innocent one) follows, only out of love and compassion for his fallen mate. This version is clearly a revision of the original, cleaned up, as it were, to ease a guilty conscience. That the weakness in succumbing to temptation is ascribed to woman is not accidental, however. She, after all, is the first object and stimulus for this most primary of all curiosities. For, if grownup men are tempted to penetrate the mystery of creation, they are merely fulfilling an infantile desire to grasp the mechanics of conception, which take place unseen in the bodies of their mothers.

From the standpoint of psychoanalysis, scientific and intellectual curiosity constitute sublimations of the child's impulse to perceive and understand what is forbidden to him. Freud (1905d, p. 156) labeled this impulse "scoptophilia." Its sublimated counterpart is called epistemophilia. Because it first arises at a developmental stage in which the child regards all *others* merely as potential sources of gratification, scoptophilia is tinged with a certain ruthlessness, if not sadism. The target of infantile and childhood curiosity has little intrinsic value. Once penetrated and forced to yield its secrets, it is invariably discarded. Greed and envy are prominent components of this pregenital curiosity. The irreducible wish is to wrest gratification from its hidden sources, to possess that which brings pleasure. Untempered as it is by concern for the well-being of others, the impulse tends to be limitless and, therefore, insatiable.

The process of sublimation ideally effects specific changes in the wish to know; the transition from scoptophilia to epistemophilia occurs within a more global growth process, which eventuates in a dramatic change of attitude towards the source of gratification. The previously discarded object begins to be valued in and for itself and not, exclusively, for its pleasure-giving contents. More concretely, the mother comes to be viewed as worthy of love and concern, apart from hedonistic expectations. In parallel fashion, the search for knowledge can now be pursued as an end in itself rather than as a means to gratification. The pleasure that previously was the goal becomes attached to the quest: *to know* becomes more important than *to have* or *to own*.

These considerations bear particular relevance to the subject at hand. The mad doctor seems frequently to begin his work with the purest of intentions. At some point in his progress, however, he appears to become contaminated with evil inclinations. Such aphorisms as "power corrupts," fail to explain the complexities that motivate the climactic change. The evil inclinations were, in fact, present at the outset, but disguised by what appears to be a single-minded dedication to the pursuit of knowledge. This dedication permits a certain "pardonable" blindness to motives that otherwise might be more clearly discernible—those that derive from the ruthless scoptophilic impulses of infancy. Thus, the old colleague was right, after all: there *are* some things that man was not meant to know. Or, more accurately, there are some things that provoke a level of curiosity that does not admit gratification.

One heretofore unsuspected reason for the universal appeal of mad doctor films is that they present to the imagination a problem that inheres in the very structure of Western scientific inquiry. Beginning with Descartes, the great scientific thinkers have always dreamed of conquering nature. The goals of modern science are prediction and control. The discoveries of "pure science" are almost invariably placed at the service of power interests. Knowing, for its own sake is currently regarded as a quirky remnant of such outmoded world views as those held by nineteenth-century Native Americans.

If scientific inquiry and its applications were informed by sublimated epistemophilic impulses rather than by the thirst for power, the objects of inquiry—the earth, people, space, the atom—would be known rather than exploited. If knowledge were more valued than the power it conveys, scientists and doctors could be trusted to explore every domain. But the researches of mad doctors, like many of our own, are impelled by the insatiable infantile craving for pleasure and dominion. Herein lies one source of their fascination. That these films culminate in the doctors' destruction and the subsequent restoration of order by the keepers of common tradition constitutes a reassurance that the more ignoble of human predilections will not get out of hand.

Apart from the impulse to possess and consume the other, there are several additional categories of pregenital yearning that play a role in the mad doctor's motivation. Of considerable importance among them is the wish to overcome the inevitable laws of nature—that is, to rule, rather than be ruled. One of the most eloquent early statements of this theme is made by Lucifer, the prototypic apostate, in Milton's *Paradise Lost* (2001). The arch-fiend avers, "It is better to reign in Hell than to serve in Heaven" (Book 1, L.263). Wishes of this variety derive, in the main, from pregenital, anal–sadistic impulses. Further evidence of the essentially anal derivation of these inclinations is to be found in the subject matter of the mad doctors' researches. They tend to be concerned with the origins of life, the attainment of immortality, and the triumph over natural forces that conduce to decay and death. This focus of interest was widespread in the Middle Ages, when alchemy was considered a respectable line of scientific inquiry. Alchemists were obsessed with the possibility of transmuting base metal into gold, a preoccupation that psychoanalysts would regard as typically anal, since minerals obtained from "the bowels of the earth" often symbolize feces at an unconscious level. Feces are a debased, repulsive form of matter, suggestive of decay and death. A means must, therefore, be found to reverse the inexorable entropic forces of nature, so as to remove the constant threat of non-being from human experience. The mad doctor, heir to the medieval alchemist, experiments with methods of creating and prolonging life. Such researchers as Viktor Frankenstein infuse life into dead matter and revel in fantasies of immortality.

There is also a pronounced antifeminine aspect to the behavior of mad doctors. They appear to suffer from a profound envy of the female generative principle, and they bend their energies to the task of freeing themselves from real and symbolic domination by women. It is women, after all, who bring forth life, and it is Mother Earth to which all life ultimately returns. The mad doctor attempts to usurp this function, to assume the prerogatives of conception and creation, and to prevent the inevitable return to the mother as represented by death. In this sense, his rebellion is not against the law of a paternal God, but, rather, constitutes a struggle to attain permanent independence from the female, and thus to avoid, once and for all, that most painful of all experiences, separation. It is significant to note, in this connection, that there has never been a memorable female mad doctor.

Returning to the account of creation in the Book of Genesis, it can be asserted that man not only ascribes his temptation to explore forbidden territory to the weakness of woman, thereby distorting the original impulse to penetrate to the core of the mystery within the female body, but that the idea that Eve emanated from Adam's rib is a similar distortion of the plain fact that man comes from woman. It must be assumed that primitive humans were unaware of the male role in conception. They must, therefore, have concluded that the generation of life was an exclusively female process. Envy and hatred of the female was doubtless predicated on this conclusion, and the wish to wrest this most crucial of all functions from her grasp probably formed the mythological basis for the universal theme of which mad doctor films are representative.

The compulsion to overthrow the maternal principle and its suffocating laws is taken a step further by certain mad doctors who, having once solved the riddle of creation, bring forth creatures of their own. It should come as no surprise that, in the first instance, these creatures are male (e.g., Frankenstein), because the impulse to create them is floridly narcissistic. Eventually, however, the doctor seeks to create or to control females, too. This development is an expression of the infantile narcissism that aims to engender a perfect, all-giving, never frustrating object that, in contrast to the too human and fallible mother, will minister to every wish and need, both expressed and latent. Such a Pygmalion attitude is characteristic of the mad doctor's penchant to form a world in which all objects, animate and inanimate, exist only for the aggrandizement and gratification of the master. Accordingly, its roots are exposed simply as the ruthless inclinations of "His Majesty, the baby." To play God is, when all the frills and fictions are seen through, nothing more than to establish a contained universe with the self at the center, a self that is protected from all pain and treated to all pleasures, one that corresponds in every particular to the infantile state which Freud called "the purified pleasure ego."

An interesting sidelight on the mad doctor theme is the career of Freud, himself. In a significant sense, Freud had the makings of a quintessential mad doctor. He began his career in partnership with Josef Breuer, an older colleague who withdrew from the dangerous researches into the secrets of the mind when he sensed the power of the forces involved, and feared he would be overwhelmed by them. It requires no great stretching of the imagination to conjure a picture of the frightened Breuer saying to his younger colleague, "There are some things, Freud, that man was not meant to know." Had not Freud already demonstrated a singular preoccupation with the idea of unlimited pleasure, combined with a rash disregard for scientific method, and a willful ignoring of possibly dangerous consequences in his experiments with cocaine? And was he not motivated by a seemingly boundless, yet baseless, ambition which, when thwarted, made him bitter? The ingredients were all there. The question, however, is why was Freud not a mad doctor? Why, when confronted with the evidence that led him to the discovery of that most effective tool for controlling and influencing others, the transference, did he reject the power it conferred on him, in favor of *knowing*?

The question is difficult to answer, but it does seem likely that, as he matured, Freud came to understand the distinctions between the pregenital uses of knowledge for the purposes of control and exploitation and the more civilized connotations of *knowing*, as an activity to be valued in its own right. A central concept related to, and perhaps emerging from, this realization was that of abstinence. What Freud discovered was that the precondition for knowing another human being is the renunciation of power over him. In the end, then, his curiosity seems to have gotten the better of him: he sacrificed the certainty of pleasure for the possibility of knowing more about the human condition at its depths.

In this respect, Freud represents an example of a would-be mad doctor who was privileged to penetrate the most profound mysteries because he gave up the wish to use them for his own enhancement. The rich insights that he brought back from his foraging in the nether regions of human experience enable those who came later to grasp the reasons for the world's fascination with mad doctors.

REFERENCES

Alighieri, D. (1951). *Cantica 1, Hell (L'Inferno)*, Dorothy L. Sayers (Trans.). Harmondsworth: Penguin.

Almodóvar, P. (Director) (2002). *Talk to Her* (Film). Spain: El Deseo, Antena 3 Televisión, Good Machine.

American Psychiatric Association (1980). *Diagnostic and Statistical Manual of Mental Disorders DSM-III*. Washington DC: American Psychiatric Association.

American Psychiatric Association (1994). *Diagnostic and Statistical Manual of Mental Disorders: DSM-IV*. Washington, DC: American Psychiatric Association.

Arendt, H. (1978). *Eichmann in Jerusalem: A Report on the Banality of Evil*. New York: Penguin.

Aristotle (1961). *Poetics*. New York: Hill and Wang.

Aristotle (2015). *Organon*. Accessed at: http://plato.stanford.edu/entries/aristotle-logic/ on March 12, 2016.

Bausch, P. (1998). Masurca Fogo, a dance piece.

Bion, W. R. (1961). *Experiences in Groups and Other Papers*. London: Tavistock.

Blake, W. (1982). The Marriage of Heaven and Hell. In: N. Frye (Ed.), *Selected Poetry and Prose of Blake*. New York: Modern Library.

Boswell, J. (1872). *The Life of Samuel Johnson, LL.D., with His Correspondence and Conversations Volume 3*, E. Malone (Ed. and Illus.). New York: Routledge.

Bram, C. (1995). *Father of Frankenstein*. New York: Dutton.

Brok, A. (2006). Some remarks on attachment, desire, and assumptive relationships. Paper presented to a Section I, Division 39 (the division of Psychoanalysis of the American Psychological Association) Symposium: Seattle, WA.

Brooks, M. (Director) (1993). *Robin Hood: Men in Tights* (Film). Brooksfilms, Twentieth Century Fox Film Corporation.

Brown, N. O. (1959). *Life Against Death: The Psychoanalytical Meaning of History*. Middletown, CT: Wesleyan University Press.

Bryant, P. (1958). *Two Hours to Doom*. London: T.V. Boardman.

Buckle, H. T. (1858). *History of Civilization in England*. London: John W. Parker and Son.

Bunyan, J. (2004). *The Pilgrim's Progress from This World to That Which Is to Come*; and *Grace Abounding to the Chief of Sinners*, J. F. Thornton, S. Bunyan, & J. B. Varenne (Eds.). New York: Vintage.

Chase, D. (Director) (2000). *The Sopranos*: Big Girls Don't Cry; D-girls (Television Series), HBO Original Programming, Brad Grey Television and Chase Films (Exec. Prod.).

Coen, J., & Coen, E. (Directors) (1990). *Miller's Crossing* (Film). Circle Films, Twentieth Century Fox Film Corporation.

Coleridge, S. T. (1967). Biographia literaria. In: D. Perkins (Ed.), *English Romantic Writers* (pp. 448–491). New York: Harcourt, Brace & World, Inc.

Coleridge, S. T. (1968). *The Rime of the Ancient Mariner*. In: M. H. Abrams, E. T. Donaldson, H. Smith, R. M. Adams, S. H. Monk, G. H. Ford, & D. Daiches (Eds.), *The Norton Anthology of English Literature* (*Volume 2, revised*) (pp. 215–231). New York: W. W. Norton.

Condon, B. (Director) (1998). *Gods and Monsters* (Film). USA, UK: Lions Gate Films, Showtime Networks, Flashpoint (I).

Conrad, J. (2008). *Heart of Darkness and The Secret Sharer*. New York: Signet Classics.

Cooper, M. C., & Schoedsack, E. (Directors) (1933). *King Kong* (Film). USA: RKO Radio Pictures.

Coppola, F. F. (Director) (1972). *The Godfather* (Film). USA: Paramount Pictures, Alfran Productions.

Coppola, F. F. (Director) (1974). *The Conversation* (Film). USA: The Directors Company. The Coppola Company, American Zoetrope.

Curtis, J. (1998). *James Whale: A New World of Gods and Monsters*. Boston: Faber and Faber.

Desilu Productions (1951–1957). *I Love Lucy* (Television show). USA: Distributors, Columbia Broadcasting System.

Dickens, C. (1996). *A Tale of Two Cities*. New York: Chelsea House.

Dirks, T. (1996–2002). Primary characteristics and conventions of film noir. Accessed March 21, 2003 at: www.filmsite.org/filmnoir.html.

Dostoyevsky, F. (1992). *Notes From the Underground*. New York: Dover Publications.

Eissler, K. (1971). *Discourse on Hamlet and "Hamlet*. New York: International Universities Press.

Eliot, T. S. (1950a). The Love Song of J. Alfred Prufrock. In: L. Untermeyer (Ed.), *Modern American Poetry: Mid-Century Edition*, (pp. 398–401). New York: Harcourt Brace.

Eliot, T. S. (1950b). The Hollow Men. In: L. Untermeyer (Ed.), *Modern American Poetry: Mid-Century Edition* (pp. 414–415). New York: Harcourt Brace.

Eliot, T. S. (1950c). The Wasteland. In: L. Untermeyer (Ed.), *Modern American Poetry, Mid-Century Edition* (pp. 402–414). New York: Harcourt Brace.

Ellenberger, H. F. (1970). *The Discovery of the Unconscious*. New York: Basic Books.

Eyre, R. (Director) (2007). *Notes on a Scandal* (Film). UK: Fox Searchlight Pictures, DNA Films, UK Film Council.

Fairbairn, W. R. D. (1952). *Psychological Studies of the Personality*. London: Routledge & Kegan Paul.

Fancher, H., & Peoples, D. (1980). *Blade Runner*. Screen Play. Accessed at http://scribble.com/uwi/br/br-Script.html on March 21, 2003.

Ferguson, F. (1949). *The Idea of a Theater*. Garden City, NY: Doubleday Anchor Books.

Fitzgerald, F. S. (2003). *The Great Gatsby*. New York: Scribner.

Fleming, V., & Cukor, G. (Directors) (1939). *The Wizard of Oz* (Film). USA: Warner Brothers.

Fonteyne, F. (Director) (1999a). *An Affair of Love* (Film). France: ARP Sélection, Artémis Productions, Canal+.

Fonteyne, F. (Director) (1999b). *Une Liaison Pornographique* (Film). France: ARP Sélection, Artémis Productions, Canal+.

Frankenheimer, J. (Director) (1962). *The Manchurian Candidate* (Film). USA: M. C. Productions. United Artists.

Freud, S. (with Breuer, J.) (1895d). *Studies on Hysteria. S. E.*, *2*. London: Hogarth.

Freud, S. (1905c). *Jokes and Their Relation to the Unconscious. S.E.*, *8*: 1–247. London: Hogarth.

Freud, S. (1905d). *Three Essays on the Theory of Sexuality. S.E.*, *7*: 123–246. London: Hogarth.

Freud, S. (1907a). Delusions and dreams in Jensen's *Gradiva. S.E.*, *9*: 1–96. London: Hogarth.

Freud, S. (1910h). A special type of choice of object made by men. *S.E.*, *11*: 163–176. London: Hogarth.

Freud, S. (1912e). Recommendations to physicians practising psychoanalysis. *S.E.*, *12*: 109–120. London: Hogarth.

Freud, S. (1912–1913). *Totem and Taboo. S. E.*, *13*: vii–162. London: Hogarth.

Freud, S. (1919h). The 'uncanny'. *S. E.*, *17*: 217–256. London: Hogarth.

Freud, S. (1920g). *Beyond the Pleasure Principle. S. E.*, *18*: 7–64. London: Hogarth.

Fried, W. (2010). Transference as a device for facilitating attention. *Psychoanalytic Review*, *97*: 483–493.

Garcia, R., Levi, H., & Bergman, N. (Directors) (2008–2011). *In Treatment* (Television series). USA: Sheleg, Closest to the Hole Productions, Leverage Management.

George, P. (1958). *Red Alert.* New York: Ace.

Goethe, J. W. (1993). *Faust.* A. Hayward (Trans.). Oxford: Woodstock Books.

Gray, T. (1964). Elegy Written in a Country Churchyard. In: O. Williams (Ed.), *The Immortal Poems of the English Language* (pp. 187–190). New York: Washington Square Press.

Hartmann, H. (1958). *Ego Psychology and the Problem of Adaptation*, D. Rapaport (Trans.). New York: International Universities Press.

Hayford, H., & Parker, H. (Eds.) (1967). *Moby Dick.* New York: W. W. Norton.

Hemingway, E. (1955). *Men without Women.* New York: Scribners.

Hippocrates (1996–2016). http://www.phrases.org.uk/.

Hitchcock, A. (Director) (1960). *Psycho* (Film). USA: Shamley Productions.

Hook, H. (Director). (1990). *Lord of the Flies* (Film). USA: Castle Rock Entertainment, Jack's Camp, Nelson Entertainment.

Huston, J. (Director) (1987). *The Dead* (Film). Channel 4, Delta Film, Liffey Films.

James, H. (2011). *The Beast in the Jungle*. New York: Penguin.

James, W. (1890). *Principles of Psychology*. Cambridge, MA: Harvard University Press.

Joyce, J. (1944). http://theliterarylink.com/joyce.html.

Joyce, J. (2009). *Ulysses: With a New Introduction by Enda Duffy*—An unabridged republication of the original Shakespeare and Company edition. Mineola, NY: Dover.

Kafka, F. (1963). *The Penal Colony; Stories and Short Pieces*, W. Muir & E. Muir (Trans.). New York: Schocken.

Kafka, F. (1992). *The Castle*, W. Muir & E. Muir (Trans.). New York: Everyman's Library.

Kafka, F. (2016). "The meaning of life is that it stops": attributed to Kafka. Accessed at: www.goodreads.com/author/quotes/5223.Franz_Kafka

Kennaway, J. (1956). *Tunes of Glory*. London: Putnam.

Kermode, F. (1966). *The Sense of an Ending*. New York: Oxford University Press.

Kiarostami, A. (Director) (2010). *Certified Copy* (Film). Italy: MK2 Productions, BiBiFilm, Abbas Kiarostami Productions.

Kovel, J. (1989). *The Radical Spirit: Essays on Psychoanalysis and Society*. New York: Free Association.

Kramer, S. (Director) (1952). *High Noon* (Film). USA: Stanley Kramer Productions. Distributors: United Artists.

Kubrick, S. (Director) (1964). *Dr. Strangelove* (Film). USA: Columbia Pictures Corporation, Hawk Films.

Laughton, C., & Mitchum, R. (Directors) (1955). *Night of the Hunter* (Film). USA: United Artists (A Paul Gregory Production).

Leonard, H. (Ed.) (2007). When Johnny Comes Marching Home. In: *Folksongs in Recital: 14 Concert Arrangements by Richard Walters*. Milwaukee, WI: Hal Leonard.

LeRoy, M. (Director) (1931). *Little Caesar* (Film). USA: First National Pictures.

Lewin, B. D. (1950). *The Psychoanalysis of Elation*. New York: W. W. Norton.

Lewin, B. D. (1955). Dream psychology and the analytic situation. *Psychoanalytic Quarterly*, 24: 169–199.

Lewis, S. (1998). *Babbitt*. New York: Bantam.

Lewis, S. (2006). *Babbitt*. The Project Gutenberg EBook of Babbitt, by Sinclair Lewis Release Date: February 11, 2006 [EBook #1156].

Lombardi, V. (Football Coach). (n.d.). Accessed at http://izquotes.com/quote/346861 on March 12, 2016.

Lovejoy, A. O. (1972). *The Great Chain of Being.* Cambridge, MA: Harvard University Press.

Magritte, R. (1929). Ceci n'est pas une pipe; *The Treachery of Images.* http://collections.lacma.org/node/239578

Marvell, A. (1989). To His Coy Mistress. In: B. Barnet, M. Berman, & W. Burto (Eds.), *An Introduction to Literature* (9th edn) (pp. 478–479). Glenview, IL: Scottt, Foresman.

Maslow, A. H. (1964). *Religions, Values, and Peak Experiences.* London: Penguin.

McCluhan, M. (1964). *Understanding Media: The Extensions of Man.* San Clemente, CA: Mentor [reprinted Cambridge, MA: MIT Press, 1994].

McDougall, J. (1980). *A Plea for a Measure of Abnormality.* New York: International Universities Press.

Melville, H. (2014). Bartleby the Scrivener. In: The Project Gutenberg ebook, *The Piazza Tales* by Herman Melville. Release Date: May 18, 2005 [ebook # 15859] Most recently updated: September 6, 2014.

Miller, A. (1989). *Death of a Salesman.* In: B. Barnet, M. Berman. & W. Burto (Eds.), *An Introduction to Literature* (9th edn) (pp. 1025–1111). Glenview, IL: Scott, Foresman.

Milton, J. (2001). *Paradise Lost and Paradise Regained.* New York: Penguin.

Mitchell, S. (Trans.). (2000). *Bhagavad Gita, a New Translation.* New York: Harmony.

Moore, M. (1970). Poetry. In: L. Untermeyer (Ed.), *Modern American Poetry: Mid-Century Edition.* New York: Harcourt Brace.

Neame, R. (Director). (1960). *Tunes of Glory* (Film). UK: Janus Films, United Artists, Knightsbridge Films.

Nichols, M. (Director) (1967). *The Graduate* (Film). USA: Mike Nichols/ Lawrence Turman Productions. AVCO Embassy Pictures: United Artists International.

O'Neill, E. (1957). *The Iceman Cometh* (Play). New York: Random House.

Oxford Dictionaries Language Matters (2016). English definition of "fey". Oxford University Press. Accessed at: www.oxforddictionaries.com

Parker, R., & Charles, H. (1939). *We'll Meet Again.* Accessed at: www. chaseside.org.uk/sheet_music/30s/wellmeetagain.html

Pascal, B. (2009). On Reading for Philosophical Inquiry: A Brief Introduction. Accessed at: http://philosophy.lander.edu/intro/articles/pascal-a.pdf on March 5, 2016.

Pound, E. (c. 1921). https://leisureguy.wordpress.com/2015/04/10/ulysses-still-outrageous/

Redding, O. (1998). Try a little tenderness. In: *Dreams to Remember: The Otis Redding Anthology* (sound recording). Los Angeles, CA: Rhino.

Reitman, J. (Director) (2009). *Up in the Air* (Film). USA: Paramount Pictures, Cold Spring Pictures, DreamWorks Pictures.

Robinson, E. A. (1950). John Gorham. In: L. Untermeyer (Ed.), *Modern American Poetry: Mid-Century Edition* (p. 129). New York: Harcourt Brace.

Sartre, J.-P. (1938). *La Nausee.* Paris: Gallimard.

Schrödinger, E. (1935). Die gegenwärtige Situation in der Quantenmechanik [The present situation in quantum mechanics]. *Naturwissenschaften,* 23(48): 807–812.

Scorsese, M. (Director). (1990). *Goodfellas* (Film). USA: Warner Bros. (presents) (A Time Warner Co.) (an Irwin Winkler Production) (as Warner Bros. Production).

Scott, R. (Director), Fancher, H., & Peoples, D. (Writers) (1982). *Blade Runner: Director's Cut* (Film). USA: The Ladd Company.

Shakespeare, W. (1957). *Hamlet.* New York: Washington Square Press/ Pocket Books.

Shakespeare, W. (1958). *Hamlet.* In: L. B. Wright & V. A. LaMar (Eds.), *The Folger Library Shakespeare* (pp. 1–147). New York: Washington Square Press/Pocket Books.

Shakespeare, W. (1989). Macbeth. In: B. Barnet, M Berman & W. Burto (Eds.), *An Introduction to Literature* (9th edn) (pp. 821–892). Glenview, IL: Scott, Foresman.

Shakespeare, W. (2004). *King Lear.* New York: Simon and Schuster.

Shelley, M. W. (1992). *Frankenstein: Complete Authoritative Text With Biographical and Historical Contexts, Critical History and Essays from Five Contemporary Critical Perspectives / Mary Shelley,* J. Smith (Ed.). Boston, MA: St. Martin's Press.

Silverman, B. (Transcriber) (n.d.). *Blade Runner Screenplay from 1982 Theatrical Release.* Accessed March 12, 2003 at: http://scribble.com/ uwi/br/script-19800724.txt

Silverstein, J. (2015). Mobster funeral featuring "Godfather" songs, horse-drawn carriages, flowers thrown from helicopter horrifies Rome officials. *New York Daily News,* updated Friday, August 22, 2015.

Sosa, T. M. (1954). Cucurrucucu paloma. Editorial Mexicana De Musica Int. S.A. (Emmi)

Spielberg, S. (Director) (2001). *A. I. Artificial Intelligence* (Film). USA: Warner Brothers.

Spielberg, S. (Director) (2002). *Minority Report* (Film). USA: Twentieth Century Fox and Dreamworks.

St. Aubyn, E. (2012). *Some Hope* [The Patrick Melrose Novels]. New York: Picador.

Stoller, R. (1975). *Perversion: The Erotic Form of Hatred,* New York: Pantheon.

Stoller, R. (1979). *Sexual Excitement, Dynamics of Erotic Life.* New York: Pantheon.

Sun-tzu ping fa (2001). *The Art of War: A New Translation.* New York: Random House.

Swift, J. (1940). *Gulliver's Travels: An Account of the Four Voyages into Several Remote Nations of the World.* New York: Heritage.

Swift, J. (2009). *A Modest Proposal and Other Writings.* New York: Penguin.

Tennyson, A. (1933). "Tithonus." In: G. M. Miller (Ed.), *The Victorian Period* (pp. 74–76). New York: Charles Scribner's Sons.

The New Oxford Annotated Bible with the Apocrypha (1973–1977). Genesis (pp. 1–50). New York: Oxford University Press.

Thomas, D. (1971). *The Poems of Dylan Thomas.* New York: New Directions.

Updike, J. (1960). *Rabbit Run.* New York: Alfred A. Knopf.

Whale, J. (Director) (1931). *Frankenstein* (Film). USA: Universal Pictures (a James Whale Production).

Whale, J. (Director) (1935). *The Bride of Frankenstein* (Film). USA: Universal Pictures (a James Whale Production).

Whale, J. (Director) (1936). *Showboat* (Film). USA: Universal Pictures (a James Whale Production).

Williams, A., & Martin, G. H. (Trans.) (2002). *Domesday Book: A Complete Translation.* London: Penguin.

Winnicott, D. W. (1953). Transitional objects and transitional phenomena: a study of the first not-me possession. *International Journal of Psychoanalysis, 34:* 89–97.

Woolf, V. (1985). *Moments of Being* (2nd edn), J. Schulkind (Ed.). New York: Harcourt Brace, Jovanovich.

Yeats, W. B. (1983a). The Second Coming. In: R. Finneran (Ed.), *The Poems: A New Edition* (pp. 187–188). New York: Macmillan.

Yeats, W. B. (1983b). The Statues. In: R. Finneran (Ed.), *The Poems: A New Edition* (pp. 336–337). New York: Macmillan.

Yeats, W. B. (1983c). The Circus Animals' Desertion. In: R. Finneran (Ed.), *The Poems: A New Edition* (pp. 346–348). New York: Macmillan.

Yeats, W. B. (1983d). Lapis Lazuli. In: R. Finneran (Ed.), *The Poems: A New Edition* (pp. 294–295) New York: Macmillan.

Zimbardo, P. G. (1971). The power and pathology of imprisonment. *Congressional Record* (Serial No. 15, October 25, 1971). Hearings before Subcommittee No. 3, of the Committee on the Judiciary, House of Representatives, Ninety-Second Congress, *First Session on Corrections, Part II, Prisons, Prison Reform and Prisoner's Rights: California.* Washington, DC: U.S. Government Printing Office.

INDEX